THE NORMAN CONQUESTS

Table Manners

A COMEDY IN TWO ACTS

by Alan Ayckbourn

SAMUEL FRENCH, INC.

45 WEST 25TH STREET   NEW YORK 10010
7623 SUNSET BOULEVARD   HOLLYWOOD 90046
LONDON   *TORONTO*

THE NORMAN CONQUESTS, by Alan Ayckbourn. "Table Manners," "Living Together," and "Round and Round the Garden." Directed by Eric Thompson; setting and lighting by Robert Randolph; costumes by Noel Taylor; stage manager, Milt Commons. Presented by Lester Osterman, Richard Horner, in association with Martin Richard Richards and Victor D'Arc, Robert Fryer, James Cresson and Michael Codron. Opening night was December 7, 1975 at the Morosco Theater, 217 West 45th Street.

THE CAST

NORMAN .... Richard Benjamin

ANNIE .... Paula Prentiss

TOM .... Ken Howard

SARAH .... Estelle Parsons

REG .... Barry Nelson

RUTH .... Carole Shelley

ACT I

The dining-room. Saturday, 6 p.m.

It is a fine evening, the sun streams through the french windows of the room. There are four chairs with a solid table, a sideboard, two window-seats and a couple of easy chairs. The room is large and high-ceilinged, and like the rest of this Victorian vicarage-type building, badly needs redecorating

As the CURTAIN *rises, Annie in a baggy cardigan, jeans and raffia slippers, enters with a flower vase of water. She thumps this down in the middle of the table, picks up the roses which lie beside it and drops them into the vase. She gives the whole lot a final shake and that, as far as she is concerned, concludes her flower arrangement*

Sarah (*off*) Hallo! Hallo, we're here!

Sarah enters. She wears a light summer coat and dress. She is breathless

Annie Sarah!

Sarah (*embracing her*) Annie dear . . .

Annie Good journey?

Sarah Oh, yes, yes, not too bad. Reg drove far too fast as usual but we got here—oh, it's lovely to come down. I've been looking forward to this week-end away from it all for weeks. Week-end? It's barely a day. You've no idea how that dreary little house of ours gets me down.

Annie Oh, it's not bad.

Sarah Try living there sometime. Not a decent shop, not a cinema, not even a hairdresser—except some awful place I can't go into because of the smell. I said to Reg, for goodness' sake you're an estate agent, surely you can get the pick of anywhere and then we finish up in somewhere like that. You're so lucky, Annie, you have no idea. Just to see a tree once in a while and the birds—I really miss it. Now then, how are you, let's look. Oh, Annie darling, you look just the same. Your hair . . .

Annie (*self-consciously smoothing her tangle*) I know—I haven't brushed it today. I washed it, though, this morning.

Sarah What's the good of washing it if you don't brush it. It's like a gorse bush.

Annie Well, nobody sees it. The postman, the milkman, couple of cows and Mother.

Sarah And Tom.

Annie Oh, yes. Tom.

Sarah You mustn't forget Tom. And how's Mother?

Annie No better, no worse. She hasn't felt like getting up, not for weeks . . .

Sarah Well, you should make her. She needs to.

Annie Old Wickham says if she doesn't want to, don't make her.

Sarah Wickham? Oh, yes, I've never really cared for him. His eyes are too close together. Still, I suppose he's all right as a doctor. He must be better than ours. I mean, this business with my back was practically criminal.

Annie Your back?

Sarah Surely I wrote and told you? I'm sure I did. I was so upset I wrote to everybody.

Annie Oh, yes.

Sarah Annie, I must buy you a new jumper, remind me.

Annie I'm attached to this one.

Sarah I should think you are—you were wearing it at Christmas. We'll have to chisel it off you . . . Mmm, lovely flowers. Now tell me. Where are you going?

Annie When?

Sarah For your week-end, where are you going?

Annie Well . . .

Sarah Oh, come on. Don't be so secretive.

Annie Well—I was going to Hastings.

Sarah Oh, lovely! Hastings is gorgeous. I think I was there with Reg just before we were married. There's a heavenly little pub some-where . . .

Annie No, well I couldn't get in at Hastings.

Sarah Couldn't get in?

Annie No, it was all booked. I forgot it was summer.

Sarah Oh. Yes. Well, where are you going?

Annie I rather fancied East Grinstead.

Sarah East Grinstead?

Annie Yes.

Sarah What an extraordinary idea. What on earth made you choose there?

Annie Well, it sounded—interesting.

Sarah Yes, I suppose it is. I've never heard of anybody having a holiday in East Grinstead. I suppose they do—but I've never heard of anybody.

Annie Well, I am.

Sarah Yes. I think I'd have almost preferred Eastbourne but . . . (*Displaying her outfit*) Do you like this?

Annie Super.

Sarah (*taking off her coat, touching the back of the chair for dust, then putting the coat over it*) It was like a tent on me when I bought it, but I had it altered. I'm rather pleased. Now, you're to leave everything to me. I'm taking over. Just tell me what pills and potions Mother has and when she has them and then off you go.

Annie I've written it down somewhere. I'll show you. The only difficult things are her drops.

Sarah Oh well, if they're difficult Reg can cope with them. He's going to do most of the running up and down stairs anyway. I mean, this is a a holiday for me, too. She's his mother. He can do something for her for a change.

Annie How is he?

Sarah Reg? (*With a big sigh*) Oh well, he's still Reg you know. I've tried, God knows I've tried, but he'll always be basically Reg. You'll know, he's your brother after all. There are times when I think he's sleep-walking. I have to force him to make an effort. Heaven knows how he runs a business. I'd certainly never let him sell a house of mine.

Annie I've left you a cold supper.

Sarah Oh, you shouldn't have bothered.

Annie Well, I knew you wouldn't want to be . . .

Sarah You shouldn't have bothered.

Annie I left it all out for you on the——

Sarah You really shouldn't have bothered.

Annie —kitchen table.

Sarah Lovely.

Annie I was just laying things in here.

Sarah Oh, there's no need for that. We'll eat with our fingers. We're on holiday, for heaven's sake.

Annie We do have knives and forks. (*She takes two sets of knives, forks and spoons from the sideboard to the table*)

Sarah I'll find them, don't bother. Now please, just get changed and go.

Annie Okay. (*She starts to move to the door*)

Sarah Oh. I nearly forgot. How's Tom?

Annie Tom? Oh, fine. I think.

Sarah Still seeing a lot of him?

Annie Oh, yes. He's generally around. When he's not out curing his sick animals. He's here at the moment, actually. The cat's got something wrong with its paw.

Sarah (*arranging the flowers*) It must be fascinating being a vet. It's a pity in a way he's not a proper doctor.

Annie He is a proper doctor. He just prefers animals to people.

Sarah That came from the heart.

Annie No. He just likes animals. Don't think he's very fond of our cat, but he likes most animals.

Sarah Yes, he's a bit—heavy going, isn't he? I've always found him a trifle ponderous. Perhaps it's shyness.

Annie No, I think he's probably ponderous.

Sarah So he hasn't—er—shown any more interest?

Annie In what?

Sarah Well, you. At Christmas, we thought he was beginning to sit up and take notice of you just a little. Pricking up his ears.

Annie Like a mongrel with a pedigree bitch.

Sarah Yes, well . . .

Annie Honestly, stop trying to pair us off. He just comes round when he's bored, that's all.

Sarah A man doesn't spend as much time as Tom does round here without having a very good reason. Believe you me. You don't have to be psychic to know what that is.

Annie Well, if it's that he's never asked for it and even if he did he wouldn't get it. So I don't know why he bothers. (*She sets out the knives and forks*)

Sarah Annie! You're getting dreadfully coarse.

Annie Oh, you're just a prude. (*She takes out two side plates, two napkins and two rush mats, and sets them on the table*)

Sarah No, I'm not a prude. No, I've never been called that. You can't call me a prude. That's not fair, Annie. I mean, I don't care for smutty talk or dirty jokes. I just don't find them funny. Or particularly tasteful. But that isn't being a prude. That's normal decent behaviour which is something quite different.

Annie Yes.

Sarah I won't have the television set on at all, these days.

Annie Anyway, all that happens is that Tom comes round here like he has done for years. I feed him. He sits and broods. Sometimes we talk. That's all.

Sarah Talk about what?

Annie (*disarranging the flowers as she moves around the table*) Oh, super exciting things like does the kitchen ceiling need another coat and distemper and hardpad and foot and mouth and swine vesicular disease. Then I pot Mother and retire to bed—alone—itching.

Sarah Oh.

Annie And count diseased sheep crashing headlong into the gate. Look for all I know he may be passionately in love with me. He may be flashing out all sorts of secret signals which I just haven't noticed. But he's never even put a hand on my knee. (*Reflecting*) God forbid.

Sarah But you're fond of him?

Annie He's—very kind. Yes, I like him a lot. I sometimes miss him when he's not here. I suppose that means something.

Sarah Yes. You see, I was rather hoping—I know it's wicked of me—I was rather hoping that you were both planning to go off for this week-end together.

Annie Oh. No.

Sarah You're not, are you?

Annie (*uneasily*) No. Not at all.

Sarah Are you sure?

Annie Of course I'm sure.

Sarah You're looking very shifty.

Annie I'm not. Honestly. No. Stop it.

Sarah Stop what?

Annie Looking at me like that.

Sarah Like what?

Annie Like that. Stop it.

Sarah You're a dreadful liar.

Annie I'm not.

Sarah Listen, if you are, there's no need to keep it a secret from me. I mean, you said I'm a prude but I've just proved I'm not, surely? I mentioned it first. I think it's splendid. I think if you and Tom were to get away from this house, away from Mother and everything—it's the best thing you could do. It's what you both need. (*She kisses her*) Very sensible.

Annie Yes.

Sarah Have a lovely time. I only wish it were me. Not with Tom, of course. But I think that's what we all need now and then, don't we? A nice dirty week-end somewhere. Oh, it's so exciting. I am pleased you're doing it. I think the best bit is waking up in the morning in a strange room and finding some exciting-looking man beside you and— you've got a double room?

Annie It's a bit more complicated than that.

Sarah Oh? How do you mean? You haven't got a double room?

Annie No, it's just . . .

Sarah What? You're not pregnant?

Annie No.

Sarah Oh, thank God.

Annie No, it's just—oh golly, I didn't mean to tell you.

Sarah Tell me what?

Annie It's awfully sordid. You're sure you want to hear?

Sarah Of course, I want to hear.

Annie It'll shock you.

Sarah My dear, I've been married for eight years. I've had two children. I think I've just about seen everything there is to see. I defy you to shock me. I honestly defy you.

Annie Well. Last Christmas, when you were all here . . .

Sarah Yes?

Annie You and Reg and Ruth and Norman. And then you and Reg left early . . .

Sarah Because Denise didn't want to miss her dancing classes—yes?

Annie And then after that, Ruth was ill . . .

Sarah Or so she said.

Annie Well, she was flat on her back with something for a week and that left Norman and me—more or less to cope. Tom was in Scotland on a course.

Sarah Yes?

Annie Anyway.

Sarah I'm beginning dreadfully not to like the sound of this one little bit.

Annie Anyway. Golly, I'm getting dreadfully hot.

Sarah Go on. What?

Annie Well, you know Norman, he's . . .

Sarah Yes, I know Norman very well.

Annie He's not a bit like Tom. I mean, just the opposite to Tom. Norman doesn't bother with secret signals at all. It was just wham, thump and there we both were on the rug.

Sarah Rug?

Annie Yes.
Sarah Which rug?
Annie The brown nylon fur one in the lounge . . . (*She starts to giggle*)
Sarah (*irritated*) What is it? Why are you laughing?
Annie (*unable to control herself*) Does it matter which rug?
Sarah I don't think it's funny.
Annie No, nor do I. I'm sorry—it's just I'm so embarrassed—oh, gosh . . .
Sarah Annie, pull yourself together.
Annie (*helplessly*) Yes . . .
Sarah (*thumping the table*) Annie, what happened on the rug?
Annie Everything happened on the rug.
Sarah Does Ruth know?
Annie No.
Sarah Or Tom?
Annie No. (*Drying her eyes*) Oh, dear . . .
Sarah Well, I blame Norman. That is absolutely typical—fur rug!

This starts Annie off again

It's just the sort of thing . . . Annie, will you stop making that ridiculous noise—typical behaviour.

Annie blows her nose

Is that it? Was that the only occasion?
Annie Oh, yes. Ruth got better and they both went home.
Sarah I suppose it could have been worse. That poor woman. I mean, I don't have a lot of time for Ruth, as you know. Personally, I find her snide little remarks, her violent ups and downs just too much to cope with. I know she's your sister, I'm sorry for talking like this. However, I would not wish my worst enemy married to a man like—not even Ruth. Heaven knows why they married. Never understood it. What did she see in him?
Annie Norman says it was uncontrollable animal lust that drew them together.
Sarah Norman told you that?
Annie Yes. He says it's died out now. They are like two empty husks.
Sarah Yes. Hardly surprising. Well, believe me, you're well clear of that, dear. You're well clear of that one.
Annie You don't think I should then?
Sarah What?
Annie Go.
Sarah Go where?
Annie This week-end.
Sarah This week-end?
Annie With Norman. To East Grinstead.

A pause

Sarah You were planning to go with Norman to East Grinstead?

Annie Yes. He couldn't get in anywhere else.

Sarah You're not serious?

Annie Yes.

Sarah But how could you even think of it?

Annie He asked me.

Sarah What has that to do with it?

Annie Well, I wanted a holiday . . .

Sarah Yes, but—this wouldn't be just a holiday. I mean, I mean, you just don't go off on holiday with your sister's husband.

Annie It was only a week-end. I needed a holiday.

Sarah Well, you could have gone on your own.

Annie (*slightly angry*) I didn't want to go on my own. I'm always on my own.

Sarah But did you realize what you would be getting yourself into?

Annie Well—the way Norman put it—it sounded simple. Just a week-end.

Sarah Norman will put it any way which suits Norman. Did you think of Ruth? And Tom?

Annie Oh, to hell with Tom. He could have asked me if he'd wanted to, but he didn't. If I wait to be asked by Tom, I won't even get on an old folks' outing.

Sarah Well, what about Ruth?

Annie That's up to Norman. He wrote to me and then he phoned and asked me and I suddenly thought, well yes—I think, actually if I'm being really truthful and, knowing Norman, I didn't think it would ever happen.

Sarah You were certain enough about it to get Reg and I down. We've had all the trouble of having to take the children to their grandparents so that we wouldn't have to bring them down here because we knew they would disturb Mother. I've had all the trouble of delegating responsibility for the Bring and Buy Sale which I'm sure will be a disaster because I'm the only one among them with any sort of organizing ability. And Reg has had to cancel his golf.

Annie I'm sorry. I've been feeling sick all morning. I'm sorry.

Sarah Yes, well I'm sure we all are.

Annie Well . . . (*She moves to the door*)

Sarah Where are you going?

Annie I don't know. I was just—I don't know.

Sarah I think it's just as well we are here. You quite obviously need a rest. Now, I want you to sit down here and leave everything to me.

Annie No, it's all right, I . . .

Sarah And let's get this quite clear to start with. You are not going anywhere. Not while I'm in this house.

Annie What about my week-end?

Sarah You can have your week-end here. Reg and I will cope. That's what we came down for. You can rest. You can certainly forget the idea of going anywhere with Norman. That's final. You're staying here.

Annie Yes. I rather thought I would be.

Sarah What you need is rest.

Tom enters from the garden

Tom Ah.
Sarah Tom! How nice to see you, Tom. (*She shakes Tom's hand*)
Tom Hallo, Sarah. Keeping fit?
Sarah Tom, I've just been saying I think Annie's honestly been overdoing it.
Tom Really? Do you think so?
Sarah You really must take more care of her, Tom. We all expect you to keep an eye on her, you know, when we're not here.
Tom Do my best.
Sarah She's rather your responsibility.
Tom Yes, can't have that. Been trying to get that cat out of the tree. Your cat's gone up a tree, Annie.
Annie Oh.
Sarah Anyway, Annie's just decided she's not going away this week-end. She's going to stay here and have a good rest.
Tom Septic paw, you know.
Sarah And Reg and I will be here to look after her.
Tom That's good news. Aren't you going then?
Annie No.
Sarah With your help, of course, Tom. You must stay for supper.
Tom Supper?
Sarah Mustn't he, Annie?
Annie Why not.
Tom Save me opening a tin at home.
Sarah Lovely. Now, I must just pop up and see Mother. Then I'll come down and organize everything. Leave it all to Reg and me. Where is Reg? I asked him to bring the cases in ages ago.
Tom I left him in the garden.
Sarah What's he doing in the garden?
Tom Nothing much. Just talking to Norman.
Sarah Norman? Norman is here?
Tom Yes.
Sarah Norman is here, under this roof?
Tom No, he's in the garden. We were chatting away.
Sarah Oh, my God. Chatting about what?
Tom Various subjects. Cats. And his pyjamas.
Sarah Pyjamas?
Tom Yes, he was showing them to me.
Sarah Do you mean he's wearing them?
Tom No. He was just generally waving them about.
Sarah Tom, stay here with Annie. Don't move. Stay here. I'll be back.

Sarah hurries out to the garden

Tom Did you know Norman was here?
Annie Yes. I saw him earlier.

Tom Oh. Were you expecting him?
Annie Not really, no.
Tom Ah. Well. (*He stares out of the window*)
Annie (*in frustration*) Oh.
Tom Put your feet up.
Annie What?
Tom I should put your feet up.
Annie (*rising and going to the sideboard*) No. Not at the moment. (*She gets out the cruet, two more mats, knives, forks and spoons, and a biscuit tin*)
Tom I'm a bit worried about that paw, you know.
Annie Paw?
Tom On the cat. Needs looking at. (*Moving in Annie's way*) Does he have a name, by the way?
Annie What? No. Just cat. (*She moves round Tom to the table and lays it*)
Tom That's all right, I don't suppose he minds. Preferable to Oscar or Herbert or something. He probably wouldn't answer to it if he had one. Cats' names are more for human benefit. They give one a certain degree more confidence that the animal belongs to you. Of course, they never do. Cats belong to no-one but themselves.
Annie Oh, I'm so stupid . . . (*She bangs down the cutlery*)
Tom All right?
Annie Yes. I just feel such a fool.
Tom Oh. Not much answer to that, is there. (*Picking up the biscuit tin*) Mind if I have a water biscuit?
Annie Have the lot.
Tom No. Just one. It'll spoil my dinner. Ah, high baked . . .
Annie Tom . . .
Tom (*crunching*) Um?
Annie What did you think when I said I was going away this week-end?
Tom Well, I don't know. I suppose I thought—you were going away this week-end. (*Holding out the tin*) Want one?
Annie (*irritated*) No . . .
Tom They're a bit stale. No, it did occur to me you might have liked someone to come along with you . . .
Annie It did?
Tom And then I thought, well, probably not.
Annie Why? What on earth made you think I wanted to go off and sit in some dreary hotel room on my own?
Tom Yes, it did seem rather odd, I must say.
Annie How long have you known me?
Tom Oh—years . . .
Annie Years. And in all that time have I ever even hinted that I'd like to go off on my own?
Tom Not as far as I know.
Annie (*angrily*) Then why the hell should I suddenly decide to do it now?
Tom Well, I don't know. Simmer down.
Annie Why didn't you say—Annie, will you be all right on your own?

Would you like company? Someone to come along, too? Someone to talk to? Why didn't you think of saying it? Just once.

Tom Oh, come on . . .

Annie Or was the whole prospect just too awful?

Tom No . . .

Annie Well, then?

Tom You should have said something. You should have asked me along. I'd've come. You should've asked me.

Annie (*weakly*) Oh, dear God. Yes, I'd have had to have done.

Tom Don't blame me.

Annie I'm not blaming you. Oh—nun's knickers!

Tom Language. You're getting awfully het up. I should put your feet up.

Annie I don't want to put my bloody feet up.

Annie stamps out

Tom gazes after her, slightly puzzled. He helps himself to another biscuit, then puts the tin on the table. Reg is heard calling from the garden

Reg (*off*) Annie, Annie, Annie!

Reg bursts in from the garden

Where is she then? Where's that little sister of mine. (*Seeing no-one but Tom*) Oh. Where is she?

Tom No idea. Kitchen, possibly.

Reg Ah. He's a laugh, you know.

Tom Who?

Reg Norman. Goes on and on. Don't know what he's talking about. Makes me laugh, though. I don't care, I like him. She doesn't but I do. Women don't, you know. Not many women like him. Don't know why. Sarah can't bear him. Won't have him in the house. Nor will his wife. (*He laughs*)

Tom I think Annie gets on all right with him.

Reg Ah well. Annie. (*He smiles affectionately*) She's something special. You'll be all right with her, Tom. Take my word. If you decide to marry any of us, marry her. Not that I'm saying you should but if you did. Mind you, you can't marry Ruth and I don't think you'd fancy me, so there's not much choice, is there? (*He laughs*)

Tom Um. (*Thoughtfully*) They're all a bit peculiar at the moment.

Reg Who are?

Tom The women. All on edge, for some reason.

Reg The women are restless tonight, eh? Full moon.

Tom Eh

Reg Probably a full moon. (*He bays like a hound and laughs*)

Tom No. Something startled them.

Reg Norman. Or mice. One or the other. I hear Annie's not going now.

Tom Apparently not.

Reg Could have had my golf. If I'd known. Never mind. Better go and see Mother in a minute. Sarah's up there at the moment. I'll wait till she comes down. Two of them, too much of a good thing. I'll put it off as long as I can. Mother always says the same thing. What did you go and marry her for? Biggest mistake of your life. You'll live to regret it. Trouble is, I can never think of a convincing answer. (*He laughs*) She's probably right. I mean, there are compensations. Children—sometimes. Even Sarah—sometimes. But when I sit here in this house and listen to the quiet. You know, I wonder why I left. I had my own room here, you know. All my books, my own desk, a shelf for my hobbies. I'd sit up there in my school holidays—happy as a sandboy. I'd make these balsa wood aeroplanes. Dozens of them. Very satisfying. Mind you, they never flew. Soon as I launched them—crack—nose dive—firewood. But it didn't really matter. It was a hell of a bore winding them up, anyway. I built one for the kids the other day. They didn't really take to it. Where's the guns, Dad? Where are the bombs then? (*He shakes his head*) Oh well, what do you expect.

Tom No, you see—I think I've stopped her from going.

Reg Who?

Tom Annie.

Reg You have?

Tom Yes ...

Reg Hope we'll get some dinner soon. I'm getting peckish. (*He takes a biscuit from the tin, leaving the lid off*)

Tom You see, she didn't want to go on her own.

Reg On holiday? Ah well. Who does?

Tom She was rather expecting me to offer to come, too.

Reg Oh. You should have been in there—like a shot, eh?

Tom Yes.

Reg While you had the chance. These are stale.

Tom Now, I've gone and upset her.

Reg Oh, dear.

Tom I've never been very good at that sort of thing. Always seem to miss the moment.

Reg That's how it goes, isn't it?

Tom Yes. I've let her down. I can feel myself doing it while I'm doing it. I suppose I'll have to find a way of making it up.

Reg I shouldn't bother. It'll blow over. Wait for the new moon.

Sarah enters from the house

Tom picks up some cutlery from the table

Sarah What are you doing in here?

Reg Oh. I beg your pardon. Is the dining-room closed? (*He laughs to Tom*)

Sarah Where's Annie?

Reg Getting us something to eat, I hope. Slaving over a hot stove.

Sarah She is not. Anyway, it's a cold meal. Where is she?

Reg I don't know.

Sarah You haven't left her in the living-room with Norman.

Reg Possibly. What's wrong? He's all right, he won't bite her.

Sarah Oh, my God.

Reg Tom'll inject her for rabies, won't you, Tom?

Tom I'll go and look for her if you . . .

Reg Inject her for rabies.

Sarah No, Tom, stay where you are. Reg.

Reg What?

Sarah Go and see if they're in there.

Reg Why don't you?

Sarah Because I'd rather you did, please.

Reg I'm not interested if they're in there. It doesn't matter to me if they're in there or not. You're the one who's interested if they're in there.

Sarah (*sharply*) Will you please do as I ask for once. Besides it'll look much more natural.

Tom I say, what's going on?

Sarah (*soothingly*) Nothing to worry about, Tom, nothing at all.

Reg I don't think it'll look more natural. I mean, what's natural about me walking in there, having a look and then walking out again.

Sarah Well, pretend you've gone to fetch something. Use your imagination, for heaven's sake.

Reg All right. All right. What am I supposed to be fetching?

Sarah I don't know. Anything.

Reg (*moving to the door and then pausing*) What's all this about a cold meal? What sort of cold meal?

Sarah Cold meat and salad. Now, go on.

Reg If there's one thing I can't stand when I'm hungry it's salad.

Reg goes out to the house

Sarah He's a difficult man. (*She takes the cutlery from Tom and replaces it*) He is such a difficult man. Ask him to do a simple thing for you and there's a twenty-minute argument. Did you talk to Annie? (*She rearranges the flowers*)

Tom Yes.

Sarah Did she—say anything?

Tom She—told me the reason why she'd planned the whole week-end. Why it had fallen through.

Sarah Oh. (*She pats his hand*)

Tom I could kick myself for being so slow off the mark.

Sarah You mustn't blame yourself.

Tom I'm afraid I do, rather.

Sarah I don't see why. I mean, you weren't to know that . . .

Reg enters with a waste-paper basket

Reg Yes, they're in there.
Sarah What's that?

Tom takes a fork from the table and wanders to the window

Reg Waste-paper basket, isn't it?
Sarah Couldn't you have found something a little more natural?
Reg What did you expect me to bring back? A bloody grand piano? (*He sits in the easy chair with the basket on his knee*)
Sarah Right, Tom.
Tom Um?
Sarah I think it's high time you went in and said your piece.
Tom Really?
Sarah Told them where you stand.
Tom Me?
Sarah Make sure Norman knows.
Tom Norman?
Sarah You'll lose your chance if you don't do it soon.
Tom (*baffled*) Oh, yes.

Reg bays like a hound

Sarah What are you doing?
Reg Nothing. Full moon, that's all. Full moon. (*He nods and winks at Tom*)
Tom Ah.

Sarah takes the fork from Tom and pushes him out

Tom goes out bewildered

Reg drums on the basket

Sarah I think this may have worked out for the best. Might even stir Tom into action, you never know. You haven't been eating these biscuits?
Reg I squelched through a couple.
Sarah You'll spoil your meal.
Reg Oh yes. All that lovely lettuce.
Sarah You and your stomach. I'd rather hoped I was in for a quiet week-end for once. It seems it's not to be. Look at these forks, they haven't been cleaned since we were last here. It's a crying shame. All this silver. (*She takes a duster from the sideboard and vigorously polishes the cutlery*)
Reg Are we staying or going?
Sarah We can hardly go home.
Reg I thought the whole point of our being here was to look after Mother but if Annie's going to be here . . .
Sarah I don't know about being here to look after Mother. We need someone here to look after her.
Reg She's managed up till now. There's Tom.
Sarah Oh, Tom. There's no point in relying on him. I mean, he's pleasant

enough, but I don't think he's quite all there. That's a terrible thing to say, but look at the way he's behaved. Mind you, she does precious little to encourage him. How is she going to attract any man looking like that, let alone Tom.

Reg She's all right. Leave her alone.

Sarah Do you realize what would happen if I did?

Reg She can manage.

Sarah I take it you've gathered what's going on in this house?

Reg What?

Sarah Where have you been for the last hour?

Reg What do you mean, where have I been? You know where I've been. I've been here, waiting for something to eat.

Sarah Norman had planned to take Annie away to a hotel this week-end.

Reg Norman?

Sarah Yes.

Reg With Annie?

Sarah Yes.

Reg Was she the one he was taking to East Grinstead?

Sarah (*impatiently*) Of course she was.

Reg gives a yell of delight

(*When this has died down, coolly*) Frankly, Reg, I think there's something mentally wrong with you. I think you ought to see someone. I'm being serious. How you can take so little interest in your own family, your own sister.

Reg Oh, Sarah, come on. (*He puts the waste-paper basket down and rises*) Sit down. You've done nothing but run round and round. I think it's funny, I can't help it.

Sarah You're the same at home. Exactly the same.

Reg Oh, now, come on . . . (*He moves away*)

Sarah Yes, you can walk away but it's always left for me to deal with, isn't it? It's left for me to apologize to people for you. It's left to me to explain why you walk straight upstairs as soon as anyone comes to visit us.

Reg They're your friends.

Sarah It's me that's left looking stupid in front of the headmistress when you forget the names of our own children . . .

Reg That was only once.

Sarah They run wild those children. You've done nothing for them. Nothing at all. If I didn't get them food, they'd starve, if I didn't buy them clothes, they'd be naked—you sit in that room, which I spend my whole life trying to keep tidy, fiddling with aeroplanes and bits of cardboard and now you can't even be bothered with your own sister . . .

Reg Sarah, please, would you kindly stop talking.

Sarah No, I will not stop talking.

Reg You have talked at me since I got up this morning—you have talked at me over breakfast . . .

Sarah It happens to be the only way I can get through to you . . .

Reg You talked solidly in the car for an hour—nearly causing us to have
   a very serious accident . . .
Sarah Which was entirely your fault.
Reg And ever since we've been here, you haven't stopped for a second.
   Now, for the love of God, shut up.

A slight pause

Sarah (*stopping polishing and sitting at the table*) I will not be spoken to
   like that. (*Tearful now*) I will not have you raising your voice to me like
   that. Just who do you think it is you're talking to?
Reg I think, like you, I'm talking to a brick wall. I'm going for a walk.
Sarah (*hysterically*) All right, go. Go on then. Go, you beastly little man.

*Sarah snatches up the biscuit tin from the table and hurls it at Reg. It hits
the sideboard, biscuits fly in all directions*

Reg Sarah!

Sarah sits sobbing. Reg stands uselessly

   Annie comes in from the house

Annie Oh.

Reg starts to pick up the biscuits

Reg Biscuits.
Annie (*moving to him*) Oh, yes. (*Helping Reg*) Here, let me . . . (*Mouthing to
   Reg*) What's the matter?
Reg (*mouthing*) Nothing.
Annie (*pointing at Sarah, mouthing*) Is she all right?

Reg shrugs

   (*Looking at Sarah and shrugging*) I'll get the dustpan.

   Annie goes out

Sarah You're contemptible.
Reg (*kneeling down to collect biscuits and tin*) You really must control that
   temper of yours, you know.

   Tom enters from the house. He pauses as he takes in the scene

*Reg, crawling on the floor, does not see him. Nor does Sarah, with her back
to him*

Sarah You are the most contemptible man I've ever known.
Reg The feeling's mutual, don't worry.

   Tom goes out to the house, looking worried

Sarah God knows what's going to happen to us. God knows.

Annie returns with the dustpan

Annie Here we are. Soon clear this up.
Reg Sorry about this.
Annie Oh well. Accidents happen, don't they.
Sarah It wasn't an accident.
Annie Oh.
Reg No. The biscuits were so stale they threw themselves off the table in desperation.
Sarah What have you decided, Annie?
Annie What? Oh well—it's all rather settled itself, hasn't it? I'm staying here, of course. (*She stands up*)
Sarah I mean, it's entirely up to you. I mean, all I was doing was trying to . . .
Annie Well, it's probably best.

Reg wanders away to the window

Sarah Tom and Norman have sorted out their differences, have they?
Annie I don't think there were any, really. Norman's getting drunk and Tom's looking thoughtful
Sarah Oh well, I've done what I can. I'm sorry, I think the man must be mentally defective. I think they both are. I'll bring some things in.
Annie It's all right, I'll . . .
Sarah No—no—no! I want to. (*Collecting her coat*) I want to bring some things in.

Sarah goes out to the house

Reg We seem to have upset your week-end. (*He sits by the table*)
Annie (*putting the dustpan by the sideboard*) Not really. It was a mad idea. (*Moving to the table, disarranging the flowers*) Rather flattering all the same. Suddenly having two men bidding for my favours. Even if they are Tom and Norman.
Reg (*chuckling*) Well, I must say—didn't know I had a sister like you. (*He pulls Annie on to his knee*)
Annie (*amused*) It's ridiculous, really.
Reg I knew one of us took after Mother—I couldn't think who it was. Certainly it wasn't me or Ruth.
Annie Not Ruth.
Reg Do you remember Mother taking us on holiday? Where was it? Weston-super-Mare. Were you old enough to remember?
Annie You mean when she picked up that sailor?
Reg Yes. He kept throwing that ball half a mile down the beach. Trying to get us all to run after it. Run along, kids. Go and fetch it. Let me talk to your mum.
Annie And Ruth wouldn't go.

Reg No, she wouldn't budge.

Annie "I'm staying here to look after Mother. I don't trust him . . ." There was Mother saying, "Run along, Ruth dear. Run along and play . . ."

Reg Then there was that Polish rear gunner.

Annie Oh God, yes. And Father suddenly came home on leave.

Reg That drain-pipe's still broken, you know. I had a look.

Annie and Reg laugh

Sarah enters with a jar of salad cream. She bangs it on the table and glares at them

Annie and Reg are silent

Sarah (*icily*) Don't let me spoil the joke. (*She takes the flowers to the sideboard and rearranges them*) I'm sure you both find me terribly amusing. I'm sure you all find me hilarious.

Annie Not at all.

Tom comes on laughing heartily, carrying a bottle

Sarah wheels on him and glares. Tom stops laughing

Sarah goes out to the house

Sarah . . .

Annie goes out after Sarah

Reg What was the joke?

Tom Nothing really. Norman told me to come in and try to jolly things up. Doesn't seem to have worked.

Reg Hardly at all.

Norman is heard singing briefly from the sitting-room—"Girls were made to Love and Kiss". Reg and Tom register

Tom Norman! (*Holding up the bottle*) I brought a bottle of this. Help wash down the radishes. Managed to salvage it. Norman's drunk most of them. (*He puts it on the table*)

Reg I didn't know we had anything like that in this house.

Tom (*getting two glasses from the sideboard*) Home-made. Mother made it last year. Just before she was ill. Annie and I bottled it. Tastes revolting but it's very potent.

Reg Carrot. Does it have to be carrot?

Tom (*opening the bottle and pouring*) Well, there's also parsnip or dandelion, but this seems to have a slightly better bouquet. The dandelion's all right but I lost the use of one side of my face for about an hour after I drunk it. (*Handing a glass to Reg*) Here, what do you think?

Reg (*tasting it*) Not bad. Not bad at all. (*Rising as it hits his stomach*) Oh, good grief.

Tom I think it's an acquired taste.

Reg You must have a stomach like a blast furnace.

Norman (*off, singing*) "Am I to blame if God has made me gay?"

Annie enters with a tray of four plates of salad which she puts on the sideboard. Sarah follows and sits at the table

Annie Grub's up. (*She puts two plates on the table*)

Reg Ah-ha, the great caterpillar hunt is on.

Annie (*bringing two glasses to the table*) No, it isn't, I washed the lettuce this time.

Reg (*moving to the table*) Oh, yes.

Annie (*bringing the remaining two plates to the table*) Well, I rinsed it under the tap. Twice. (*She sits at the table*)

Tom Shall I give Norman a call?

Sarah No.

Reg What I always say about your salads, Annie, is that I may not enjoy eating them but I learn an awful lot about insect biology. My appreciation of the anatomy of an earwig has increased enormously... (*He sits*)

Sarah Could we keep off this subject, please.

Tom Wine, Sarah?

Sarah What is it?

Tom Wine. Home-made.

Sarah Oh well, just a little.

Tom pours wine for Sarah, then for all the others

Thank you.

Tom sits and tucks his napkin under his chin. They all eat in silence

Reg Could you pass the centipede sauce, please.

Annie giggles. Sarah glares

(*Raising his glass*) Well, here's to us . . .

Sarah I think it would be fitting to drink to Annie and Tom.

Tom Really? Why is that?

Annie Because we're here.

Tom Oh, I see. I thought there was a special reason.

Sarah That's rather up to you, isn't it, Tom?

Tom Um?

Reg Cheers, anyway.

Sarah Good health, Tom, Annie.

Reg Tom and Annie.

Tom Tom and Annie.

Sarah drinks, puts down her glass.

Sarah Oh it's really rather . . .

Her stomach explodes. She lets out a gasp. Tom and Annie half rise.

Annie Sarah!
Tom All right? (*He begins to bang her back rather heartily*)
Sarah (*regaining her breath*) Yes—it took me by surprise.
Annie Yes, it tends to do that.
Sarah (*not enjoying Tom's attentions*) That will do, Tom, thank you. That will do.
Reg It'll kill off any beetles you've swallowed.
Sarah Will you stop making remarks like that.
Reg (*raising his knife by way of apology*) Sorry—sorry.
Sarah For goodness' sake. For once in this family, let's try and have a civilized meal.

They eat in silence. From a distance Norman is heard singing in the living-room. Annie, Tom and Reg hear this, catch each other's eyes and then, under Sarah's withering gaze, continue to eat. As Norman's singing becomes louder and more boisterous, Annie, Tom and Reg become helpless with stifled laughter

CURTAIN

SCENE 2

The same. Sunday, 9 a.m.

Norman is standing in his pyjamas and bare feet. He is whistling. After a moment Sarah, in a dressing-gown, enters with a tray of breakfast things which she takes to the table

Norman (*cheerfully*) 'Morning.
Sarah (*seeing him*) Oh. (*She unloads the tray, ignoring him*)
Norman Lovely morning. Hear the birds?

Sarah continues grimly with her task

Sleep well? Hope you slept well. I slept well.

Sarah goes out

Norman starts to whistle again and examines what Sarah has put on the table

Annie enters, in a dressing-gown, with another tray of breakfast things

'Morning
Annie (*seeing him*) Oh.

Annie starts unloading her tray, ignoring him

Norman Lovely morning. Sleep well, did you? I slept like a log. Must have been that wine. Wonderful. It's a rotten drink but it makes a lovely sleeping draught. I'd market it. Sleep Nature's way with our dandelion brew. Arhar . . .

Annie goes out passing Sarah coming in with the last of the breakfast things

Norman What have we got for breakfast, then? What have we got?
Sarah (*calling*) Reg! Breakfast.
Reg (*off, distant*) Right . . .

Sarah sits and starts her breakfast

Norman How's old Reg this morning? All right, is he? Sleep well, did he? I can tell you I can do with some breakfast. Missed my meal last night. Did you know that? I missed my meal. I didn't hear the dinner gong. What sort of hotel do you call this?

Annie enters

Sarah Have you taken Mother her's up?
Annie Yes.
Norman I'll sit here, shall I? All right if I sit here? Anybody any objections if I sit here? (*He is ignored*) I'll sit here.

Norman sits at the head of the table. Sarah sits at the other end with Annie close to her, isolating Norman. Norman sits whistling

Reg enters, dressed in a sports shirt and sandals

Reg (*cheerily*) 'Morning, all.
Norman 'Morning.
Reg (*his face falling*) Oh.

Reg sits next to Sarah. Annie and Reg have cereal. Sarah butters toast

Norman Well, you're a right cheery lot, aren't you? Look at you. A right cheery lot. Woo-hoo-hallooo . . . (*He waves at them*)
Sarah (*acidly*) Nobody in this house is speaking to you ever again.
Norman Oh, I see. I see. That's the way the Swiss rolls. I see. That's the way the apple crumbles, is it? Oh ho. That's the way the corn flakes . . . (*A pause. He ponders. Suddenly—sharply*) Sarah! Be careful! The butter . . .
Sarah (*alarmed*) What?
Norman Ha-ha! You spoke to me. Caught you. Caught you. (*Pause*) All right, I'll talk to myself then. (*Very rapidly, in two voices*) Hallo, Norman —good morning, Norman—how are you, Norman—I'm very well, Norman—that's good news, Norman . . .
Annie Shut up, Norman.
Norman Ha-ha! Caught you again. That's two of you. Just got to catch

old Reg now. Two out of three. Just Reg left . . . (*Slight pause*) Look out, Reg! (*No reaction*) Ah—can't catch him that way. (*Sharply*) Hey, Reg! Oh well. If that's the way it is. Don't talk to me. I don't care. Doesn't bother me. I don't know why you're all being so unsociable. All right, I had a few drinks last night. What's wrong with that? Hasn't anyone round this table ever had a drink then? Come on, I don't believe it. You've had a drink, haven't you, Reg? Ha-ha! Caught you. You spoke.

Reg No, I didn't.

Norman Ha-ha! Three to me. I've won. (*Pause*) Nothing wrong in a few drinks. Don't speak. I don't care. Going to be a pretty dull Sunday if we all sit in silence, I can tell you. Well, I'm not sitting in silence. I'll find something to do. I know, I'll go up and frighten Mother.

Sarah looks up sharply and gives him a terrible glare

Ah-ha! Nearly got you again. Is it too much to ask for something to eat?

No response

It's too much to ask for something to eat. (*He gets up and moves down the table and takes the cereal bowl that Sarah is not using*) May I borrow your bowl? That's awfully nice of you. And your spoon? Thank you. Now then, what shall I have? (*Examining the cereal packets*) Puffa Puffa Rice. Ah-ha . . . (*He returns to the top of the table, sits and fills his bowl*) No Sunday papers. Dear, dear. Ah, well I shall have to read my morning cereal. (*He laughs*) Cereal. Do we all get that? Apparently we don't. (*He reads. Suddenly violently banging the table*) Stop!

The others jump involuntarily

Stop everything. Listen. A free pair of pinking shears for only seventy-nine p and six Puffa Puffa tokens. Hurry, hurry, hurry. What's this? Is nobody hurrying? Do you mean to tell me that none of you want them? Where's the spirit of British pinking? Dead, presumably. Like my relations. (*He eats a handful of dry cereal thoughtfully*) Hang on, I've got another game. Mind reading. I'll read your minds. Now then, where shall we start? Sarah. Sarah is thinking—that noisy man up there should be home with his wife. What is he doing shattering the calm of our peaceful Sunday breakfast with his offers of reduced price pinking shears. Why is he here, shouting at us like this? Why isn't he at home, like any other decent husband, shouting at his wife? He came down here to seduce his wife's own sister. How low can he get? The fact that his wife's own sister said, at one stage anyway, that she was perfectly happy to go along with him is beside the point. The fact that little Annie here was perfectly happy to ditch old reliable Tom—without a second thought —and come off with me is beside the point. We won't mention that because it doesn't quite fit in with the facts as we would like them. And what is little Annie thinking, I wonder? Maybe furtively admiring my pyjamas, who knows? Pyjamas that could have been hers. With all that they contain. (*He sits*) "These nearly were mine." Or maybe she is thinking, "Phew, that was a close shave. I could be shacked up in some dreadful hotel with this man—at this very moment—what a lucky escape for me. Thank heavens, I am back here at home amidst my talkative family exchanging witty breakfast banter. Knowing my two-legged faithful companion and friend, Tom, the rambling vet, is even now planning to propose to me in nineteen-ninety-seven just as soon as he's cured our cat. Meanwhile, I can live here peacefully, totally fulfilled, racing up and down stairs looking after Mother, having the time of my life and living happily ever after until I'm fifty-five and fat. I'm glad I didn't go to that hotel." Well, let me tell you so am I. I wouldn't want a week-end with you, anyway. And I'll tell you the funniest thing of all, shall I?

Annie gets up and runs out

(*yelling furiously after her*) I didn't even book the hotel. I knew you wouldn't come. You didn't have the guts.

A pause

Sarah You can be very cruel, can't you, Norman?

Sarah goes out after Annie

Norman Oh, well. It's a bit quieter without those two. Hear yourself speak. Too damned noisy before. All that crunching of toast. Like a brigade of Guards marching on gravel. Well now, Reg . . .

Reg chews glumly through his cereal

(*Looking round the table*) Milk? Ah. (*He gets up*) Sugar? (*He returns with these and sits. Pouring milk over his cereal*) Nice peaceful morning. Just the two of us and—hark! the soft crackle of my Puffa Puffa Rice. 'Tis spring indeed. (*Slight pause*) I suppose you think I'm cruel, too, don't you? Well, I've damn good cause to be, haven't I? I mean, nobody's thought about my feelings, have they? It's all Annie—Annie —Annie—what about me? I was going to give her everything. Well, as much as I could. My whole being. I wanted to make her happy for a week-end, that's all. I wanted to give her . . . (*Angrily*) It was only for a few hours for God's sake. Saturday night, back on Monday morning. That was all it was going to be. My God! The fuss. What about your wife, Norman? What about my wife. Don't you think I'd take Ruth away, just the same? If she'd come. But she won't. She has no need of me at all, that woman, except as an emotional punch bag. I tell you, if you gave Ruth a rose, she'd peel all the petals off to make sure there weren't any greenfly. And when she'd done that, she'd turn round and say, do you call that a rose? Look at it, it's all in bits. That's Ruth. If she came in now, she wouldn't notice me. She'd probably hang her coat on me. It's not fair, Reg. Look, I'll tell you. A man with my type of temperament should really be ideally square-jawed, broad-shouldered, have blue twinkling eyes, a chuckle in his voice and a spring in his stride. He should get through three women a day without even ruffling his hair. That's what I'm like inside. That's my appetite. That's me. I'm a three-a-day man. There's enough of me in here to give. Not just sex, I'm talking about everything. The trouble is, I was born in the wrong damn body. Look at me. A gigolo trapped in a haystack. The tragedy of my life. Norman Dewars, gigolo and assistant librarian. What's inside you, Reg? Apart from twelve bowls of cornflakes? What do you feel with Sarah? Do you sometimes feel like saying to her, no, this is me. The real me. Look at me . . .

Reg finishes his cornflakes

Reg I'll tell you something, Norman. You're a nice bloke. You've got your faults but you're a nice bloke, but I think you must be the last person in the world I ever want to have breakfast with again.
Norman Oh.
Reg No hard feelings you understand, but . . .

Sarah enters, looking pleased

Sarah Well, Norman. A little surprise for you.
Norman Oh, yes.
Sarah Someone to see you.
Norman Ruth?
Sarah Just arrived. Isn't that nice? (*Turning to go off, calling*) Ruth!

Sarah goes out to the house

Reg (*alarmed*) Did someone say Ruth? Oh, no . . . (*He rises, snatches a piece of toast and butters it hastily*)
Norman Tell her I'm not here. Tell her I'm . . .

Ruth enters. She is yelling the end of a conversation with Annie back in the kitchen

Ruth . . . I was pulled right over to the left, there was plenty of room for him to pass me. He had yards and yards, he just . . . (*Turning into the room*) Norman? Where is Norman?
Norman Norman is here.
Ruth (*peering short-sightedly*) Norman?—Oh, there you are.
Reg (*buttered toast in hand, heading for the french window*) 'Morning, Ruth. See you later.

Reg goes out to the garden

Ruth (*continuing as if he was still in the room, fumbling in her bag*) Oh, Reg, how are you. I've been meaning to ring you but I haven't had a minute and how are those enchanting kids of yours? Little whatsername . . . ?

Norman He's gone.

Ruth (*looking up, peering round the room*) What?

Norman Reg has left the room. He's gone.

Ruth Oh. Well, I was only being polite. I haven't seen him for ages . . .

Norman You haven't seen anyone for ages. Why don't you wear your glasses?

Ruth (*sitting*) Norman, what is going on here? What are you up to?

Norman Since when have you cared what I'm up to?

Ruth Well, I don't normally. You know you're perfectly free to come and go. Not that I could stop you. But I do object to having my Saturday nights ruined by all these bizarre phone calls. First of all, you ringing up screaming drunk—and then Sarah, practically at midnight, simply demanding I come down. Now what is going on?

Norman You don't know?

Ruth No. Is there anything to eat?

Norman Sarah hasn't told you then?

Ruth All she said was that you were here and that I ought to be here, too. She sounded as if she was summoning relatives to your bedside . . .

Norman I suppose she was, in a manner of speaking.

Ruth I got quite worried.

Norman Worried? Hah!

Ruth What's that you're eating?

Norman Since when do you worry about me?

Ruth Of course I do. Now and then. Don't be tiresome. Is that cereal?

Norman Puffa Puffa rice. (*Pushing the bowl to her*) Here, have it. After all you said to me about having no love for me—no feelings for me at all?

Ruth Did I say that?

Norman You know you did.

Ruth No, I didn't.

Norman It's imprinted on my brain . . .

Ruth All I said was—is there any milk and sugar or do I have to eat these dry—all I said was . . .

Norman It's got milk on . . .

Ruth All I said was—that if you were all that unhappy with me—perhaps we ought to think of terminating our marriage . . .

Norman (*excitedly*) Terminating it? You make it sound like a legal contract.

Ruth That's exactly what it is, Norman. Don't be obtuse.

Norman Marriage is more than that!

Ruth Yes, all right, don't shout . . .

Norman Marriage is sharing and giving and—things. Is that how you've seen us for five years? A legal contract? Some marriage. No confetti, please—just throw sealing wax and red tape. Do you take this woman, hereinafter called the licensee of the first party . . .

Ruth Norman, I can't go into all this now. Is there any sugar on this table?

Norman And this man, hereinafter called the donor and sole giver . . .

Ruth Norman, darling, do see if you can find the sugar.

Norman (*rising and assembling everything in sight around Ruth*) Here. Tea, toast, marmalade, butter, knife, spoon, cup, saucer, hot water, sugar. All right?

Ruth Thank you.

Norman (*sinking back in a chair*) I don't think there's any hope for us. We're doomed.

Ruth Norman. Can we talk quietly, please.

Norman I doubt it.

Ruth This is a perfect opportunity. We're on our own. We can sit here, talk, listen to each other's point of view and try and sort things out. (*She picks up the hot water jug*)

Norman (*making an effort*) All right. All right. I'll try. (*With sudden suppressed anger*) You are pouring hot water on your Puffa Puffa rice.

Ruth (*absently*) What?

Norman I told you they had milk on already. Why do you do that? You're always doing that. Why don't you look what you're doing?

Ruth It doesn't matter.

Norman If you'd only wear your glasses.

Ruth I don't need glasses to eat cornflakes. I can see perfectly well, thank you. I just wasn't concentrating . . .

Norman We're incompatible. We're damn well incompatible.

Ruth I can see as well as you. It's only people I sometimes can't see very clearly.

Norman Our house is knee deep in unused pairs of glasses.

Ruth And most of the time that's preferable.

Norman It's like a sale at an optician's.

Ruth Norman . . .

Norman Thousands of pairs of glasses.

Ruth (*angrily*) Norman! (*Taking a breath, calmly now*) I have a great deal of work I should be doing at home. I have given that up. I have come down here because I was asked to come. I did not want to come. I want to stay as short a time as possible. Is that clear?

Norman Oh, yes. Got to get back to your work.

Ruth Yes, I do. I have two full reports that have to be in tomorrow. If they are not in, I shall proably be fired. If I'm fired, we will have no money to pay the mortgage, no money for three quarters of the gas and electricity bills . . .

Norman All right, I'm a kept man. A married ponce.

Ruth I don't mind keeping you. Not in the least. But I cannot continually chase after you all over the countryside. I just cannot spare the time, I'm sorry. As it is, you've held my career back about ten years. You interrupt me at meetings with embarrassing phone calls . . .

Norman To tell you I love you, that's all. Is that wrong?

Ruth You're continually bursting into my office when I'm seeing clients . . .

Norman My God, is it wrong to love your wife?

Ruth You behave abominably when I bring business friends home to dinner . . .

Norman (*snarling*) What do they know about love?

Ruth You have even been known to scrawl obscenities over my business papers.

Norman All right, all right. I love you. I'm sorry.

Ruth Yes, I love you too, Norman, but please leave me alone.

Norman All right. In future, I'll whisper it quietly from Brazil. Would that suit you?

Ruth All I'm saying is, please try and see my point of view. Try and consider me.

Norman I feel trapped. I'm a captive husband. That's what I am. (*He sinks his head in his hands*)

Ruth I have an awful feeling we haven't made much progress on that topic. Let's try another. What have you been doing down here to upset Sarah? I thought you had a conference.

Norman Hah!

Ruth Have you made a pass at her or something? Well, you'd better come home with me. You're not wanted here quite obviously. You can come home and mow the lawn.

Norman Mow the lawn . . . Do you want to know what I'm doing here? I'll tell you, shall I?

Ruth If you want to.

Norman I will tell you. (*He rises*)

Ruth Where are you going?

Norman Nowhere. I'm just standing up.

Ruth Well, sit down, I can't see you properly.

Norman This has to be said standing up.

Ruth What is it, the National Anthem?

Norman All right, you've had this coming . . . (*He pauses dramatically*)

Ruth Anyway, I discovered that they're what made me sneeze.

Norman What are?

Ruth My glasses. Whenever I wear them, I sneeze and my eyes run, so I can't see anything with them on anyway. I think they press on my sinus passages.

Norman Vanity, that's what it is.

Ruth It is not vanity. I am not vain.

Norman Staring at yourself in the mirror all day long. Tarting yourself up for these so-called business associates.

Ruth And I do not stare at myself in the mirror. For one thing I can't see myself properly without my glasses, and because I can't bear looking at myself in glasses because I look so terrible in them, I never look at myself at all.

Norman Do you want to hear what I have to say or don't you?

Ruth Yes, all right. Just don't say I'm vain.

Norman It concerns you, you know.

Ruth It usually does.

Norman There is someone else.

Ruth What?

Norman Whilst you have been engrossed in your financial wizardry—rigging the books for corrupt capitalist companies . . .

Ruth Norman . . .

Norman I very nearly, but for the grace of God and unforseen circum-
stances, went off with another woman.

Ruth You did?

Norman Yes.

Ruth Seriously?

Norman Yes. I thought better of it in time. Thank heavens. Told her, I
wouldn't. But that was the reason behind this week-end. We had
planned to go off together.

Ruth For good?

Norman No—probably not . . .

Ruth Well, for how long?

Norman Till Monday.

Ruth Oh, I see. I thought you were a bit odd lately.

Norman Odd?

Ruth Well—quieter than usual. Who was it you were going with?

Norman Does it matter?

Ruth No. Since you didn't even go.

Norman Do you want to know?

Ruth Not if you don't want to tell me.

Pause

Norman You want to know though, don't you?

Ruth No, not really.

Pause

Norman I'll tell you, shall I?

Ruth You might as well.

Norman Annie.

Ruth Annie?

Norman Yes.

Ruth Oh, Norman . . .

Norman I thought that would shake you.

Ruth I don't think I even believe you.

Norman It's true.

Ruth Not Annie. She's far too sensible.

Norman We had planned a week-end together.

Ruth You and Annie?

Norman (*irritated*) Yes.

Ruth Where?

Norman East Grinstead.

Ruth (*staring at him a second and then bursting into laughter*) Oh, my
God . . .

Norman Don't laugh. It's true.

Annie enters with a tray

Just the two of us together.

Ruth (*laughing uncontrollably*) I have never heard anything so funny.

Annie I'll clear this later, I'm sorry . . .

Norman Annie! (*To Ruth*) Why won't you believe me? We were going away—together . . . (*Grabbing Annie*) Annie, you tell her, you tell her . . . You'd have lost me for ever, do you know that?

Annie (*pulling away*) Oh, Norman . . .

Ruth (*drying her eyes*) I'm sorry—it's just East Grinstead . . . (*She starts laughing again*)

Norman All right, go on, laugh. We're in love.

Norman strides across to Annie seizes her and her tray rather awkwardly and clasps her to him

Don't you care? We're in love . . .

Sarah comes in with a second tray. She stops in the doorway

Annie (*struggling, muffled as she is clasped to Norman's bosom*) Norman, don't . . .

Norman We're in love . . .

Ruth continues to laugh. Sarah surveying the scene, looks on horrified

CURTAIN

ACT II

Scene 1

The same. Sunday, 8 p.m.

Annie is discovered putting knives and forks away in the sideboard. Norman creeps in

Norman (*in a whisper*) Annie.
Annie (*jumping*) Oh, don't do that. Frightened me to death.
Norman (*whispering*) Hallo.
Annie (*whispering*) Hallo. What are you doing?
Norman (*whispering*) Wanted to see you alone.
Annie (*whispering*) Why are we whispering?
Norman (*whispering*) Them.
Annie (*normally*) They can't hear us.
Norman (*loudly*) Oh, Annie, I need you. (*He moves to her*)
Annie Ssh. (*She pulls away*) Norman . . .
Norman What's wrong?
Annie Nothing. Just don't . . .
Norman Why not? Have you gone off me?
Annie Well, slightly—no. You know . . .
Norman What do you mean, slightly?
Annie (*confused*) Oh . . .
Norman What?
Annie Well, it's ridiculous now. Tom's here. Ruth's here. Stop playing games.
Norman Oh, it's a game now, is it? When we planned this week-end it was no game. It was going to be an adventure. An experience for both of us.
Annie But we didn't plan to spend it here, did we? Anyway, it's all gone wrong. Everybody knows, including Ruth.
Norman Ruth? I wouldn't worry about her. She laughed. Can you imagine that, laughing . . .
Annie She was right. It was absurd. I don't think Tom's laughing, mind you.
Norman Tom. Who cares what he thinks.
Annie I do.
Norman You do?
Annie Yes.
Norman I thought he didn't matter to you.
Annie I never said that.
Norman You implied . . .

Annie No.

Norman What about me? I mean, us?

Annie (*sharply*) What about us, Norman?

Norman I see. That's me finished with, is it? As far as you're concerned. Chucked away like an empty bottle. That's my lot.

Annie Yes.

Norman God, you're cruel.

Annie Yes.

Norman I expect it's because of last night, isn't it?

Annie Not really.

Norman That's why you're angry with me. Because I got drunk. But I got drunk because of you, don't you see? I was unhappy so I got drunk. I'm sorry.

Annie Doesn't bother me.

Norman I got disgustingly drunk.

Annie You can get as drunk as you like, it doesn't bother me.

Norman Oh, great. Would you mind if I dropped dead?

Annie That's entirely up to you.

Norman Oh, fine. That's fine. (*He ponders*) You're getting bitter. Did you know that? You used to be innocent and pure and fragile.

Annie Oh, balls. I'm sorry, Norman, but balls. You do talk rubbish. No-one can spend five years looking after that cantankerous woman upstairs and remain innocent and pure. And after lugging her in and out of bed single-handed, day in day out, I'm the last person in this world you'd call fragile. I mean, look at me, Norman, do I look even remotely fragile?

Norman I meant mentally fragile.

Annie That sounds even worse. Makes me sound like a half-wit.

Norman I don't know what's got into you. You've been corrupted.

Annie I'm sick to death of being used, Norman.

Norman I think I must have corrupted you, somehow.

Annie You and Ruth will have to play on your own. Don't use me as ammunition.

Norman And cynical. I never thought you'd get like that. I think it's my fault. (*Pause*) So you're going back to Tom?

Annie I'm not going back to anyone. I just want to be left alone. I've had you shoving me, Sarah shoving me, Ruth sniggering. I'll be glad when you've all gone home. I really will. I'm sorry.

Norman I think I've got one of my depressions coming on again. I came in here for comfort.

Annie Well, go and see Ruth.

Norman All right. Back to the living death, eh?

Annie Oh, Norman. You make me so angry.

Norman All right. I'll go. I know when I'm not wanted. I'll go back where I'm not wanted. I'll go. Good-bye.

Annie (*infuriated, picking up the biscuit tin threateningly*) I warn you, I'll . . .

Norman Go on. Go on. What have I got to live for?

Annie screams in frustration. She bangs down the tin

Tom enters from the garden

Tom Ah.
Annie Hallo, Tom.
Tom Hallo.

They stand for a moment in silence

Norman Well, I can see I'm in the way. If you'll excuse me, I'm just off to look for a length of rope.
Annie You are not in anyone's way but your own. I'm going to start dinner. Excuse me both of you.

Annie goes out to the house

Norman It must be your after-shave.
Tom Um?
Norman That drives them away.
Tom Oh. Look here, Norman. You're a very good fellow.
Norman Thank you.
Tom I've always thought of you as a good fellow. However. This is difficult to say without hurting your feelings. I don't think you're a very good influence on Annie.
Norman Really?
Tom I've heard all about this business of your going away. I've also observed you this week-end. I don't think I like it at all. It's upsetting her and that's not right. The point is, if it happens again—well, I used to do boxing. I didn't enjoy it and I wasn't at all good. I couldn't get out of it, you see. It was compulsory at our school. But I did learn to throw a pretty useful punch. So . . .
Norman Am I being threatened?
Tom Yes.
Norman My God, I'm being threatened . . .

Sarah comes in from the house, with a duster

I am being threatened.
Sarah About time.
Norman Hah!
Sarah (*calling*) Reg!
Tom Excuse me.

Tom goes out to the garden

Norman That man's turned homicidal.
Sarah (*polishing the table*) I think as far as you're concerned, we all have to a certain extent, Norman.

Norman Sarah. You don't hate me, do you? I mean, I know perhaps you disapprove but you don't hate me.

Sarah No, I don't hate you, Norman.

Norman Thank you. Thank you for that, at least.

Sarah But I can't say I like you very much, most of the time.

Norman All right. All right, I'm going . . .

Sarah Norman.

Norman What?

Sarah Will you do something for me?

Norman What?

Sarah Will you try, just for this evening, not to start any more scenes or arguments?

Norman Me?

Sarah (*still polishing away*) I'd like, just for once, all of us to get through an evening—as a family. I don't know if you've realized it, Norman, but I have had a lot of nervous trouble in the past. And every time I come down here, I have a relapse. When I get home from this house, I find I'm shaking all over. For days. And I get these rashes up the insides of my arms.

Norman My goodness.

Sarah Now it's not fair on me, Norman. I have a family to look after, a house to run.

Norman Yes, yes of course.

Sarah Well.

Norman Yes. Your trouble is you're over-emotional.

Sarah Very possibly.

Norman You're like me.

Sarah Are you sure I am?

Norman We feel. We've got nerve-endings sticking out of our heads. We've no cynicism or scepticism to act as shock absorbers. Everything that is, that happens becomes part of us. We're probably a new race. Had you thought of that? Born too early.

Sarah All I'm saying is, if there's too much noise, I get these headaches.

Norman We're not understood. None of that lot out there understand us. They're all bogged down in their own little lives.

Sarah Yes . . .

Norman Self obsessed. Annie, Tom, Ruth—even Reg. Don't worry, Sarah.

Sarah What?

Norman This evening's going to be all right.

Sarah Is it?

Norman We'll both go flat out together to make it a success.

Sarah Oh, yes?

Norman For God's sake, this is a family. We should care. If we don't care, brothers, sisters, husbands, wives—if we can't finally join hands, what hope is there for anybody? Make it a banquet, Sarah my love, make it a banquet.

Sarah There's nothing in the larder.

Norman Improvise. We can improvise. What do we need? (*He rushes to* *the sideboard and grabs handfuls of cutlery indiscriminately from the drawer)* Knives—forks—spoons . . . (*He scatters them on the table*)

Sarah Yes, all right, Norman, I'll do it.

Norman (*producing linen*) Table napkins.

Sarah No, Norman, those are traycloths. (*She starts to lay the table*) I'll do it, don't worry, please.

Norman All right. I've started you off, I'll leave it to you. I'll go and change.

Sarah Change?

Norman For dinner.

Sarah Change into what?

Norman I'll find something. I'll improvise, Sarah, improvise. It's like an old clothes' shop upstairs.

Sarah Annie should have cleared it out. There's her father's clothes still in the wardrobe. There'll be moths.

Norman Quite right.

Norman goes to the door and passes Reg coming in

'Evening, Reg, old sport.

Norman slaps Reg on the back and exits

Reg What's up with him?

Sarah Oh, there you are. (*She replaces the cloths, then continues to set out the cutlery*)

Reg He's very cheerful. That looks ominous.

Sarah I think I've persuaded him to make an effort this evening. I think I have. Would you see if you can find the mats in the drawer.

Reg What sort of effort? (*He looks for the mats*)

Sarah To avoid hysterical scenes. To behave in a civilized manner.

Reg (*at the sideboard*) Ha—ha—ha.

Sarah I pray that for once we might get through the evening without one angry word. I want us to have a quiet meal, to be able to go into the lounge afterwards, sit down all six of us and enjoy each other's company like a family. (*She fetches glasses, napkins and side plates from the sideboard*)

Reg Are you aware who the six people are? Norman to name but five. And Ruth. That's a civil war to start with. Don't ask for the impossible. Just pray we're still alive tomorrow morning. That'll do for a start.

Sarah (*laying the table*) I mean, if a family can't care about each other, what hope is there for the rest of the—I'll never forgive you if you don't try. I mean it, Reg. I know you find it all very amusing—Ruth and Norman continually bickering, Annie behaving like a tramp . . . (*She folds the napkins into a "shape"*)

Reg What?

Sarah You've seen how she's been dressed all day. Tarted up like that, it doesn't suit her, it never did.

Reg You're always on she doesn't bother.

Sarah She doesn't have to go the other way, does she? Why can't she wear something nice and simple and—plain . . . ? All that make-up on. I mean, it's not even fashionable. Especially when you know who she's done it for.

Reg Tom, I should think.

Sarah Tom. For Norman. She's set her sights at him and he's enjoying every minute of it. Playing one sister off against the other . . . Well, any more of this and you know what'll happen? What always happens when I come down here.

Reg Oh, no? You've not got the shakes again, have you?

Sarah You ought to know me by now, Reg. I can't bear these sort of atmospheres.

Reg It's not your back, is it?

Sarah Not at the moment. But the way I've had to run round trying to cope with one crisis after another . . .

Reg Well, sit down. Have a rest for a second.

Sarah (*snapping*) How can I sit down? Be sensible. How can I possibly sit down?

Reg (*snapping back*) All right, stand up. Suit yourself. I'm only trying to be . . . You want these mats?

Sarah Yes, I said I did.

Reg (*studying them*) Marvellous, these are, every picture tells a story.

Sarah (*taking the mats and setting them out*) We're going to need two more chairs. I'm sure there used to be six of these. Heaven knows what she's done with them.

Reg All right, I'll look for chairs. Don't worry, keep calm. It'll be all right.

Annie enters

Annie Well, I've scraped together what there is. It should just about feed us all. Opened every tin we had and poured them into a saucepan. Made a sort of gluey stew. Then there's the salad we can finish . . .

Reg Oh, good grief. Not again.

Annie It works out about one lettuce leaf each.

Reg Thank heaven for that.

Sarah Well done. Didn't you have six of these chairs at one time? I'm sure at Christmas . . .

Annie Oh, yes, they fell to bits.

Sarah Fell to bits?

Annie Everything does that in this house. Woodworm or old age.

Reg You should get that treated.

Annie Old age, you mean?

Reg Ah well, I don't know about that. Father used to say, the only thing for old age is a brave face, a good tailor and comfortable shoes. Chairs . . .

Annie I should use the ones in the sitting-room. There's a couple there with legs.
Reg Right.

Reg goes out

Annie You're using the mats.
Sarah Yes, I thought we'd . . .
Annie Bit posh. We only use those on Mother's birthday.
Sarah Well, I thought we'd do something a little special since we're all here. Nice that Ruth could come.
Annie Yes.
Sarah It makes it complete. And it means that Norman won't be left out.
Annie Yes.
Sarah I really do like that dress.
Annie Thank you. It's pretty old but it's a good standby.
Sarah Yes. Anyway, I thought we'd have a really cosy family meal together. Try and make it a happy evening.
Annie Super.

Reg enters with a chair which he places down R of table

Reg Here's one of them.
Sarah We need two.
Reg All right, all right. I'm going back for the other. Tom's sitting on it.
Sarah Well, move him off it.
Reg (*going out*) You ever tried moving, Tom?

Reg goes out as Ruth enters

Ruth Somebody's saucepan seems to be getting rather agitated out there.
Sarah Did you turn it down?
Ruth No. I whispered soothing words to it. Of course, I turned it down.
Annie I'll see to it.
Sarah All right. I'll go. I'll go. (*With a glare at Ruth*) If you want something doing in this house, you might as well do it yourself.

Sarah goes out

Ruth My God, Mother's mats. Is it a birth, a death or a marriage?
Annie She's doing the lot. I mean, she's not actually doing anything but she's organizing the lot.
Ruth What on earth for, silly cow? Who's going to notice?
Annie I think this is her attempt at a grand reunion. A cosy family meal with Sarah presiding.
Ruth Oh, no. Have we all got to sit round with fixed grins? It's Christmas all over again. I thought I'd come in here so I wouldn't embarrass your fiancé or whatever he is. He can't bear to look me in the face.

Annie Poor Tom.

Ruth It was rather unfortunate. Believe it or not, I was attempting unsuccessfully to give him lessons on how to woo you. Tom being Tom assumed I was giving him lessons on how to woo me. I managed to load him all right but I pointed him in the wrong direction. It was silly of me to interfere, I'm sorry. Serves me right. I'll leave it to Sarah in future. I mean, I don't know, you may not even care for the man. You've never really said one way or the other. We've always assumed you and Tom, Tom and you. Presumably you wouldn't have him round here at all if you didn't. You do like him, don't you?

Annie Yes. I'm very fond of him.

Ruth I think he's in love with you. As far as one can fathom. It's just he's so—well, one could be nice and say deep. Except if you say someone's deep, it more or less implies there's something at the bottom. I'm not so sure with Tom.

Annie Oh, you'd be surprised.

Ruth All he needs is a shove. Somebody needs to do it. Anybody. Except Norman, that is. Whose sole advice to Tom was to throw punches at you.

Annie Norman told him to do that?

Ruth It's Norman's answer to female psychology. He's very subtle. Have you noticed? Well, you probably have. You nearly fell for it.

Annie I'm sorry. I never for a minute intended to take Norman away from you or anything.

Ruth Forget it. You couldn't possibly take Norman away from me. That assumes I own him in the first place. I've never done that. I always feel with Norman that I have him on loan from somewhere. Like one of his library books. I'll get a card one day informing me he's overdue and there's a fine to pay on him. Oh, I should have gone back to town this afternoon. I'm going to have to phone the office tomorrow and plead illness. Again. Of all the working days lost in this country over the year, half are due to strikes and illness and the other half to people chasing after Norman.

Reg comes in with the other chair, which has a low seat. He places it up
L *of table*

Reg Got it. He moved. Tom moved. Got the chair.

Ruth Have you seen Norman? I don't like it when I can't see him. Where is he?

Reg Oh, he was shouting about out there. Said something about going up to change.

Annie He's got nothing to change into.

Ruth That won't stop him. He'll probably come down in a counterpane.

Annie Oh, goodness . . . (*She starts to go out*)

Reg whistles. Annie stops and turns to Ruth
  Would you . . . ?

Ruth I'll try . . .

Ruth goes out, passing Sarah returning with a bottle of home-made wine

Sarah Don't go too far away, Ruth. Nearly ready. I've left the stew to simmer, Annie. Reg, would you call everyone. Tom and Norman.
Reg Right you are. (*Going to the door and yelling*) Tom! Norman!
Sarah (*wincing*) Please, there's no need to shout. Go and fetch them.
Reg Sorry. (*Whispering*) Tom. Norman.
Sarah Reg . . .
Reg All right. All right . . .

Reg goes out. Tom comes in from the garden

Tom Somebody call? (*Sighting the table*) Aha, this looks promising.
Sarah Nearly ready.
Tom Very smart. Napkins, mats, wine—so on.
Sarah And tonight, that wine is strictly rationed.
Tom Ah.
Sarah If you could open it, Tom, it would be most helpful.

Sarah goes out

Tom Right. (*He starts to pull the cork*) Two meals in two days. Not doing badly, am I?
Annie About average.
Tom I think I've sorted things out with Norman.
Annie Have you?
Tom Sent him off with a flea in his ear, I'm afraid.
Annie Oh. Tom . . .
Tom Um?
Annie We've all made a sort of agreement that we're going to try and not have any rows or anything tonight. It's for Sarah's sake really. A really happy meal, you know. So do your bit, won't you?
Tom What, you mean jokes and things?
Annie No, not necessarily.
Tom Oh, good. I'm awfully bad at jokes. I forget the ending.
Annie No, well—I know you never do—but don't complain or cause any trouble, will you?
Tom Lord, no. Just get my food down me. That's all I'm here for. You know me.
Annie (*doubtfully*) Yes . . .

Sarah enters with a tray of plates adorned with sparse salad, which she puts on the sideboard

Sarah Come along. It's all ready. Where is everyone? (*Calling*) Reg . . .

Reg enters from the garden

Reg Can't find either of them. (*Seeing Tom*) Ah, there you are.

Tom Hello, Reg.

Reg No sign of Norman, he's vanished.

Sarah Well, all right, we won't wait. Let's get seated. Reg, you go up the end there, would you?

Reg Up the end. (*He sits* R *end of the table*)

Sarah And Tom, you come next to me here, would you? (*She indicates the chair up* L)

Tom walks to the down L *chair and pulls it out*

Ruth enters

Ruth Norman's in the bathroom.

Sarah Oh well‚ . . .

Ruth From the sound of it, he's washing. He's so ashamed of the fact he's locked the door. (*She sits in the chair Tom has pulled out*)

Sarah Oh well, he'll be down I expect—no, not there, Ruth dear. Would you mind sitting one seat further up?

Ruth moves to the chair down R *and sits*

Ruth (*moving grudgingly*) Oh, really . . .

Annie Where am I sitting?

Sarah (*to Tom who has sat on chair vacated by Ruth down* L *and unfolded napkin*) You're here, Tom. (*Indicating the chair up* L) Sit here.

Tom rises and moves to sit, unfolding the napkin. He does not sit on this low chair until the end of the sequence

Reg (*offering Annie his own chair*) Annie, you should be sitting here. You're the hostess.

Annie (*sitting*) Right.

Sarah No, she can't sit there. She's out of order.

Reg She's the hostess. She should sit at the head.

Sarah But then we've got two women sitting together.

Ruth (*indicating down* L *chair*) I'll move back down here then. That's easy enough.

Sarah (*stopping her*) No, Ruth, no. Stay where you are.

Reg Now I'll go here next to Annie. Then it's right. (*He sits up* R)

Tom No, it's not. You're next to me.

Sarah (*getting agitated*) Now, we've got two men together. Why don't you leave it to me?

Reg It's all right, it's all right. Don't get excited. Now, Tom, you move round one and sit at the end there.

Sarah moves to the down L *place, refolding the napkin*

Tom (*going to do so*) Right-ho. (*He sits* L *and unfolds a napkin*)

Ruth Would it be easier if I ate in the kitchen?

Reg Just a second. Do you mind, Ruth, do you mind.

Sarah Don't sit there, Tom. That's my chair.

Tom Oh, I'm sorry, I thought he said . . . (*He moves one chair further round and unfolds a napkin*)

Reg Now, we want a girl over here. Ruth. Over here.

Ruth (*moving round the table to above it*) I don't want to worry you but you've got a woman at both ends of the table.

Sarah That's what I'm saying. Why won't you listen?

Reg No, no, look. We've got Ruth there—then me—then Annie—Norman over there, when he comes and Tom next to—ah, that's where we're wrong. Tom, you're in the wrong seat.

Tom (*jumping up guiltily*) Sorry. I thought she said . . .

Ruth (*moving back to the chair down* R) I am about to sit down permanently.

Sarah Reg, will you listen.

Reg Tom, you're supposed to be at the end.

Sarah Reg . . .

Tom I've just been moved from there.

Ruth I am sitting down—now. (*She sits*)

Reg Look, do as you're told and go to the end.

Tom sits L *immediately behind Sarah and unfolds a napkin*

Sarah (*screaming*) Reg, will you kindly leave this to me.

Reg I am simply trying . . .

Annie (*hissing*) Reg.

Reg What? All right, love, all right. I leave it to you. I was only trying to help. Everybody, go where Sarah tells them.

Sarah Thank you. Tom. (*She glances round the table unable to find him. Then, discovering him behind her, angrily*) You are sitting here.

Tom Aha. Back where I started. (*He sits up* L)

Sarah Reg, at the top.

Reg (*sitting*) That's wrong, you know . . .

Sarah At the top. Ruth.

Ruth I have sat down. I refuse to get up.

Annie (*hissing*) Ruth.

Sarah Ruth, you're all right where you are.

Norman enters, now dressed in an old ill-fitting suit and collar and a floppy tie. His jacket has a row of medals on it

Norman 'Evening.

Sarah (*aghast*) Norman.

Reg laughs. Sarah glares. Annie takes two plates from the sideboard for Sarah and Tom

Annie Ssh.

Reg stops laughing

Norman I heard we were dressing for dinner. Good evening. Carry on, talk among yourselves.

Norman sits between Reg at the top of the table and Tom, who is on the very low chair

Sarah No, Norman, not there.

Reg Is that my father's suit you've got on?

Norman If he was a man with extraordinary arm and inside leg measurements, yes indeed.

Annie takes plates to Norman and Reg

Sarah Norman, not there.

Norman Why not here?

Annie (*hissing*) Norman.

Sarah Because it's wrong.

Norman Wrong? Is it wrong to sit between my old pal Reg and this dwarf on my left? (*Patting the top of Tom's head*) Hallo, little chap.

Tom Hallo.

Ruth (*hissing*) Norman.

Sarah Norman!

Annie It's all right, Sarah. I'll sit here. It's fine.

Sarah But . . .

Annie brings plates for Ruth and herself and sits down L of the table

Annie This is fine.

Reg Fine.

Ruth Fine.

Tom Fine.

Sarah Oh, well. It's not correct. (*She sits L of the table*)

Norman Is this lettuce leaf all for me? I can hardly believe my good fortune.

Annie (*hissing*) Norman.

A pause

Sarah Well . . .

A pause

Reg (*suddenly*) Talking of animals . . .

People look up in surprise

Another amusing story about a vet for you, Tom.

Tom Oh.

Reg There's this Englishman and this Italian, you see, standing by a lake.

Norman That's unusual.

Reg And, anyway, they see this dog fall in the water, you see—nearly drowning—coughing and spluttering—nearly drowning.

Norman Woof—splutter splutter—woof woof.

Reg Thank you, Norman. Yes. Well, the Italian dives in, rescues the dog, brings it back to the shore, lays it out, gives it mouth-to-mouth respiration . . .

Norman Uggh.

Reg Twenty seconds, the dog's perfectly all right. The Englishman says, that's wonderful. Are you a vet? The Italian says, am I a vet? I'm a-soaking vet, what do you think? (*He laughs*)

Norman laughs. The others manage faint smiles. Silence

Norman I liked that. Subtle foreign joke. Did you get that, Tom?
Tom Yes, I think so.
Norman Thought it might have been above your head. (*He laughs*)
Annie (*hissing*) Norman.
Norman Above your head . . .
Ruth Norman.

Ruth aims a kick at Norman but kicks Reg. Reg jumps

I'm sorry.
Norman (*rising*) This lettuce is superb. Whoever cooked this has a knack with lettuce. It's a triumph. Thank you. (*He sits*)

A pause

Sarah Are you all right there, Tom? You're terribly low.
Tom No, I'm fine.
Sarah Do you want to fetch a . . . ?
Tom (*anxiously*) No, no, no.
Sarah We've been very lucky with the weather.
All Yes.
Norman True, true. (*Pause*) Could have been raining, couldn't it?
Sarah Yes.

A pause

Norman Or even snowing. (*Pause*) Snow in July. Unusual but you never know these days, do you? I mean, we must be thankful for small mercies, in my opinion. If this was Australia, this would be mid-winter. Think of that. Thick snow on the koolibah trees, koala bears rushing about in gum boots . . .
Ruth Norman, just sit quietly and enjoy your lettuce.
Norman (*in an undertone*) I'm making small talk.
Ruth Yes. Well, it's not quite small enough, dear.
Norman I can't get it any smaller. I'll swallow it.

A pause

Tom Excuse me . . .
Sarah Yes, Tom.
Tom Er—salt.
Sarah Pass Tom the salt, Norman.
Norman Salt. Certainly. Here we are, little fellow. You enjoying eating with the grown-ups, are you? Long past your bedtime.
Tom Oh, do put a bun in it, Norman, there's a good chap.
Norman A bun. I should be so lucky.
Sarah Why don't you get a cushion, Tom?
Tom (*irritably*) No.

Sarah All right, all right. I was only suggesting . . .
Tom Sorry.

A pause

Annie Everyone finished? I'll get the rest. (*She rises and starts to stack
    plates*)
Sarah Tom hasn't quite finished.
Tom All right, all right. Don't worry about me.
Ruth Do you mean to say there's more?
Annie Just some stew so called.
Ruth Well, I'll try and squeeze it in.
Annie Look, if you want to take over and try and do any better . . .
Ruth All right, sorry.
Annie Sitting there on your backside complaining.
Ruth Who's complaining? It's a feast.
Sarah (*shrilly*) Don't let's quarrel, please.
Reg Plates. Let's have the plates, everybody.

*Reg stacks his, Ruth's and Norman's plates and gives them to Annie.
Norman takes Tom's plate as he is about to take a mouthful of lettuce*

Annie Thank you. Won't be a second. (*She starts to go*)
Tom Annie . . . (*He holds out his knife and fork*)

   Annie pauses to take Tom's knife and fork, then goes out

Sarah (*in a low whisper*) Reg . . .
Reg Mm?
Sarah (*quietly*) Offer to help.
Norman (*loudly*) Offer to help.
Reg Oh, all right. Does she need it?
Sarah She's doing it all on her own.
Reg All right.

   Reg goes out

Sarah Now, would somebody like to pour us some wine?
Norman (*rising to do so*) Certainly. Certainly. My pleasure . . .
Ruth This meal is rapidly becoming unbearable.
Norman (*offering wine*) Sarah?
Sarah Just a little drop. Thank you, Norman.

Norman continues pouring wine around the table

Ruth Why don't you take a tranquillizer and go to bed, Sarah. Leave us
    to fight in peace.
Sarah Because there is no reason to fight.
Ruth None of us happen to like each other very much. I think that's a
    a very good reason.

Norman Speak for yourself. I am full of love this evening.
Ruth Just for yourself? Or is anyone else included?
Sarah Ignore her, Norman, ignore her.
Norman I will, Sarah, I will.
Tom Ah!
Norman (*sitting again, to Tom*) Hallo, Junior.
Tom I just remembered it. A joke.
Ruth Oh, God.
Sarah Oh, a joke, Tom. That's nice.
Tom Quite a funny one, really.
Norman I prefer those.
Sarah Go on, Tom.
Tom Er—well—it's about these two missionaries. And they're in Africa,
   you see and—no, three missionaries, sorry—and they were . . .
Sarah In Africa, yes.
Tom I think it was Africa. Doesn't really matter, really. Anyway . . .

*Annie enters carrying the stew in a saucepan followed by Reg with a pile
of soup plates: they put them on the table*

Annie Here we are. Thought we'd better use soup plates. It's very runny.
   It's mostly tinned soup, anyway.

Reg sits

Sarah Couldn't you have used the dish?
Annie This is all right. Nobody minds a saucepan. Just more washing up
   otherwise. Do you want to dish up or shall I?
Sarah No, no, that's all right.
Tom And there was this tribe of very wild cannibals.
Annie Cannibals? Where?
Tom In Africa, I think.
Annie What's he talking about?
Ruth He's telling us a joke.
Annie Oh, no, Tom love, you don't need to. Honestly.
Norman It's a funny one.
Sarah Quiet. Let Tom tell his joke.
Annie (*starting to dish up*) I hope there's enough to go round.
Tom And the first missionary says, look here, I'm going to try and convert
   these very wild cannibals to Christianity. You see. And off he goes—
   through the jungle . . .
Annie (*to Tom*) Can you pass this to Reg?
Norman Good health, friends.
Tom Through the jungle—for days and days . . .
Annie (*handing a plate to Ruth*) Ruth.
Reg What are these white lumps?
Annie Tinned potatoes, probably.
Reg Oh.
Annie Could be tinned pears. I lost count.

Tom And eventually he comes to this village which is full of these very
wild cannibals dancing about . . .

Norman Woolla—woolla—woolla.

Annie That's for Norman. I hope it's hot enough.

Ruth What on earth do you call this?

Annie Sloppy stew. Take it or leave it. Tom . . .

Tom (*taking his plate*) Thank you very much. And as soon as they see him,
they grab hold of him and put him in the cooking pot.

Norman This is a very tall story for a short man.

Annie Sarah—oh, I've run out. I gave Reg too much. Reg . . .

Ruth You can have mine.

Annie No, I gave Reg too much. Pass your plate down, Reg.

Reg Ah. Some more is there?

Norman No. Less.

Reg Less?

Annie I miscalculated. Sorry.

Reg Well, I didn't get all that much.

Sarah You had more than anybody else. Pass your plate.

Reg passes his plate back

I'm sorry, you were saying, Tom?

Tom Yes. And the chief of these very wild cannibals says . . .

Annie shares out Reg's helping

Annie Sorry, Reg, fair shares for all.

Ruth You're welcome to mine.

Reg We're in no danger of overeating.

Reg's plate is passed back. Annie sits

Tom I think I'm giving this story up.

Sarah You eat far too much, anyway. Do you good.

Tom Nobody seems to be listening.

Norman I'm listening, little friend.

Reg I'll be glad to get home for a meal.

Sarah It's all right for you, you don't have to cook it, do you. Think of
me for a change . . .

Annie This isn't bad, considering. Like oxtail soup with unidentified
lumps.

Sarah Think of it as a rest for me. I mean, what rest do I get at home.
Not only you to look after but the children as well.

Ruth If you didn't want children, you shouldn't have had them.

Sarah I never said I didn't want them, Ruth.

Ruth You're always making out they're some dreadful burden. Like a
penance. You never seem to enjoy them.

Sarah It's very difficult to talk to someone who's never had any children.

Ruth Through choice. Through choice.

Norman Your choice.

Ruth Certainly my choice.

Sarah And very one-sided it is by the sound of it.

Ruth No more than yours probably was. I mean, did you honestly consult Reg as to whether he wanted children?

Sarah Of course I did.

Annie Biologically impossible not to, I should think.

Reg and Norman laugh

Ruth I simply cannot bear this blind pig-headed assumption that you're a totally unfulfilled second class woman until you've had children.

Sarah I never said that.

Norman May I say a word here?

Ruth You imply it. You use those children like some awful weapon. I alone who have borne children know the true meaning of suffering.

Norman Hear! Hear!

Sarah I don't know what you're talking about. That's absolute nonsense. I mean, it's no business of mine if you choose to deny yourself one of the greatest satisfactions . . .

Ruth There you go again. Denying myself. What's the matter with the woman?

Reg Hey, hey.

Sarah I might well ask what was the matter with you?

Ruth There is nothing whatever the matter with me.

Norman May I put in a word for the rational man?

Ruth No, you may not. We've heard quite enough from you for one week-end.

Norman So much for the rational man.

Ruth By all means have your children. I'm not asking you to deny yourself, as you put it. All I'm saying is, for God's sake don't stand about looking martyred once you've had them. And don't look down your nose at the rest of us.

Sarah I'm not prepared to get into another argument over this, Ruth. You don't know what you're talking about. You never will.

Ruth She is so dogmatic. Reg, I feel sorry for you. How do you live with a woman like this who's so pig-headed? She just will not listen.

Sarah Listen . . .

Ruth She will not listen to a single word.

Sarah Will you listen to me for a minute? If I feel sorry for anyone, it's Norman.

Norman A blow for the rational man.

Sarah Have you ever consulted him? Of course you haven't. You've just gone selfishly ahead with your own career . . .

Ruth While you're busy manufacturing lots more little Reggies and Sarahs. What a wonderful contribution that is.

Sarah Oh well, if we're going to get personal.

Ruth If that isn't selfishness and conceit of the worst sort, I don't know what is. (*Banging down her spoon angrily*) And this is absolutely revolting, I don't know how anyone can eat it.

Ruth pushes her bowl angrily from her. It knocks Reg's wine glass and spills the contents over his trousers

Reg (*jumping up angrily*) Oh, for crying out loud.
Ruth I'm sorry. I'm sorry. Here . . . (*She flings her napkin at him*)
Reg Look at these trousers. Why the hell don't you watch what you're doing?
Sarah All right. Don't make a fuss.
Reg What?
Sarah Don't start losing your temper over a little thing like that.
Reg Now, don't you start on about people losing their tempers. If anyone's got a temper in this room, we know who that is.
Sarah I don't know how you have the nerve to say that.
Norman May I interrupt here?
Reg I'm going to change these. I'm soaking.
Sarah It wouldn't be surprising if I did have a temper living with you.
Norman Without displaying any prejudice, my wife is obviously to blame for this.
Ruth Norman, don't you start.
Norman She is the original irrational woman.
Annie Norman.
Reg I am going to change my trousers.

Reg goes out to the house

Norman She has no feelings of womanhood, let alone motherhood.
Annie Norman.
Ruth You really do ask for it, don't you?
Norman And you're jealous of those that have.
Annie Norman (*She rises*)
Ruth You just say one more thing, Norman . . .
Norman You've got as much feeling as a dried up tea bag.
Sarah (*shrilly*) Stop it.
Annie Norman.
Tom (*rising and pushing Annie back into her seat*) Right. That's quite enough from you.
Norman Eh?
Tom I warned you, Norman.

Tom launches an unexpected blow at Norman. Norman falls off his chair

Annie Tom!
Sarah (*drumming on the table with her fists*) Stop it! Stop it! Stop it!
Tom There.
Ruth Serve you right.
Tom I warned you. I warned him, you know.
Norman What did you do that for? (*He gets up*)
Tom I did warn you. I said if you upset Annie any more. I'm afraid I can't sit by and have her called names by you.

Norman What names?

Tom Well, you called her a—tea bag or something. That is not on. I won't have that.

Norman You fool. I wasn't talking to her.

Tom What?

Norman I was talking to my wife.

Tom Oh. Were you? Oh, that's rather different.

Ruth (*rising*) Oh, thank you. Meaning I am an old tea bag, I suppose.

Tom No, I didn't mean that.

Ruth Oh, to hell with the lot of you.

Ruth storms out to the house

Norman You great idiot.

Tom I'm very sorry. I thought you were talking to Annie.

Norman You great stupid—vet.

Tom (*trying to help him*) I really am terribly . . . Can I . . . ?

Norman Oh, go away. Just go away.

Tom (*moving to go*) Yes, yes, of course. I'm sorry. (*Turning in the doorway*) Misunderstanding, you see. Oh gosh.

Tom goes out to the house

Annie Tom—oh, Norman, how could you?

Annie follows Tom out

Sarah sits in a state near to traumatic shock. She is visibly shaking. Norman rises

Norman Lunatic . . . (*He paces about*)

Sarah This is the last time I do anything for this family.

Norman Do you know he could have killed me? If I'd fallen awkwardly. If I'd fallen that way instead of this way—I'd have broken my neck. Sobering thought. But who would have cared, Sarah? Who would have cared?

Sarah How could they? How could they do it? How could they behave like that?

Norman (*moving to Sarah*) We are misunderstood people, Sarah. Misunderstood. (*He pats her head*)

Sarah (*suddenly lunging and clinging to him*) Oh, Norman.

Norman We are definitely misunderstood.

CURTAIN

SCENE 2

The same. Monday, 8 a.m.

Annie comes in with a tray of breakfast things. She is now dressed as before in Act I, Scene 1. She starts to lay the table

Sarah comes in

Sarah Oh . . .
Annie 'Morning.
Sarah You're already doing it.
Annie Yes.
Sarah (*sitting at the table*) I was going to get breakfast.
Annie Were you?
Sarah You should have let me.
Annie It's all right.
Sarah Well, we have to be off early. We won't be needing anything very much.
Annie There isn't anything very much. Toast. Remains of the marmalade. Jam—damson, I think.
Sarah That'll do us nicely.
Annie Good. Well, it's all there. Help yourself.
Sarah I suppose I better give Reg a call.
Annie No, no, don't over-exert yourself. I'll do it.
Sarah Thank you. He's in the sitting-room, I think. He should've brought down our suitcases.
Annie Right.

Annie goes out

Sarah selects a piece of toast, examines it, finds it a little burnt and scrapes it distastefully. She sniffs the butter, finds it more or less okay. She sniffs the rather ancient looking nearly empty jar of marmalade. This she does reject. She starts spreading her toast

Norman comes in

Norman Ah-ha. Breakfast. Good morning.
Sarah (*not very warmly*) Good morning.
Norman Sleep well? (*He changes the low chair and sits above Sarah*)
Sarah No.
Norman I did.
Sarah Good.
Norman Are you angry with me?
Sarah No.
Norman This toast going free?

Sarah Yes.

Norman Cheer up, Sarah.

Sarah And what is there to cheer me up? I have never been through such a shattering week-end in my life.

Norman I'm sorry.

Sarah It wasn't all your fault. Most of it was. But not entirely.

Norman I think you ought to take care of yourself, you know.

Sarah How do I do that?

Norman Well. We don't want to lose you, do we?

Sarah I don't think some people would mind one way or the other.

Norman You find it hard to relax. That's the problem. I know that's your problem because it's my problem. As we were saying last night—I don't know how you keep going. I mean, I don't have two children and a house to run—and a husband. I've just got me. That's bad enough.

Sarah I should imagine it would be.

Norman But two children . . .

Sarah You try explaining that to some people. Your wife, for example.

Norman Oh well, quite. She wouldn't understand.

Sarah She doesn't.

Norman I know as far as I'm concerned the whole thing's a miracle. Children. Just to think of the act of actually having them. Amazing. Damn it, Sarah, you've got something to be proud of, haven't you? If you look at it this way, just by having those kids of yours, you have been responsible for two miracles.

Sarah Well, it's not that difficult.

Norman It is to me. I've never done a miracle. I saw a film on it once. Childbirth. It came out as far as its ears and I fainted. Mind you, you wouldn't have been looking at it from that angle.

Sarah I was unconscious. Both times.

Norman Ah.

Sarah It's afterwards, looking after them.

Norman Quite.

Sarah That's when it's difficult.

Norman You must be exhausted. How old are they now?

Sarah Denise is seven and Vincent's five.

Norman Seven years you've been looking after children. Would it be impertinent to ask when you last had a holiday?

Sarah I hoped this week-end was going to be one but . . .

Norman No, be honest with me, Sarah. When did you last have a holiday?

Sarah I do not remember. It was too long ago.

Norman Exactly. (*Pause*) You ought to get away. You need to. Can't you say to Reg—Reg, I need a couple of days even. I must get away.

Sarah He wouldn't take me away. And who's going to look after the children. It's no holiday with them. It was difficult enough this week-end. I was racing round organizing things, arranging this . . .

Norman Go on your own. Leave him to look after them, for a change.

Sarah Him?

Norman Why not?

Sarah Huh! (*Pause*) I wouldn't want to go on my own. What fun is it on your own?

Pause

Norman I'll take you if you like.
Sarah I beg your pardon?
Norman I said I'll take you.
Sarah On holiday?
Norman If you'd like to go.
Sarah You must think I was born yesterday.
Norman I would.
Sarah You really have got a nerve.
Norman I only offered. All right, all right . . .
Sarah First Ruth, then Annie, then me.
Norman Oh, Annie. That was different.
Sarah How?
Norman Well, it was. This would just be a holiday. For you. I'd take you round, give you a good week-end. Wouldn't you enjoy that?
Sarah No.
Norman Somewhere nice. What about Bournemouth? Ever been to Bournemouth?
Sarah I have no desire to go to Bournemouth.
Norman I've made you the offer. I leave it to you. Think about it. It would be above board. I'd book us a nice hotel. Breakfast in bed—separate breakfast. Separate beds. Separate rooms. Can't you imagine it? We'd wake up in the morning, side by side, in our separate rooms and there's the sea. And we've got all day to look at it. No children to worry about. No husband to run after . . .
Sarah Just you.
Norman Just me. I'd like to see you happy, Sarah.
Sarah Yes?
Norman Yes. Is that wrong of me? To want to see you happy?
Sarah Depends how you do it.
Norman I'd give you a good time. We'd have fun. Have you ever been to Bournemouth? It's a great place. Laugh a minute.
Sarah I can just see us going.
Norman I'd very much like to make you happy.
Sarah Pass the jam, would you?
Norman Here.

Reg enters

Reg Ah, now where's the food? (*He sits*)
Sarah Where have you been? (*She pours a cup of tea for Reg*)

Norman passes the tea to Reg

Reg What do you mean, where have I been?
Sarah Annie was supposed to call you ages ago.

Reg She did. I popped upstairs to Mother.

Sarah What for?

Reg With the magazines. I took your magazines up to Mother. You told me to. Oh, Tom's here. Told you he'd come back, didn't I? Well, he's come back. I was looking out of the sitting-room window and there he was, lurking in the garden. I told him I thought he was a cat burglar. (*He laughs*) I'm ravenous.

Sarah Yes, all right. Well, just get yourself a piece of toast. We've got to go.

Reg What's the hurry?

Sarah Because I want to get home early.

Reg What on earth for? The children aren't due back till this afternoon.

Sarah And before that, I have to go over the house from top to bottom, don't I? You may not realize it but the house has to be cleaned. It doesn't clean itself.

Reg You cleaned it before we left. Nobody's been in it since. How can it have got dirty?

Sarah It's been standing for a whole week-end. Anyway, Mrs Bridges comes to clean tomorrow. I want to make sure it's clean before she does.

Reg Oh, I give up. (*He rises and moves to the toast-rack*).

Sarah You don't understand. You never will.

Reg Not much here to eat, is there?

Sarah That's because there's nothing in the house.

Reg You're telling me. I've been starving since Saturday morning. On a diet of lettuce and soup.

Sarah Now you know what it's like with nobody running after you, don't you?

Reg Oh, blimey, look at this toast, all cold and flabby. I can't eat this.

Sarah Well, go and make some fresh.

Reg Where?

Sarah In the greenhouse. Where do you think?

Reg All right, all right. You're in a really cheery mood this morning, aren't you?

Reg goes out, taking the toast-rack

Norman (*confidentially*) It's difficult, isn't it? I know. Difficult sometimes . . . (*He pats her hand*)

Sarah Don't do that.

Norman Why not?

Sarah Because you're covering me in jam.

Norman Sorry. (*He licks the jam off her hand*)

A pause

Sarah Were you just thinking about my health?

Norman When?

Sarah When you mentioned about this holiday? Did you want to take me away just for my health?

Norman Well, that came into it. There might be any number of reasons. I'm easy. (*He smiles*)

Sarah So long as I know. (*She smiles*)

Ruth enters

Ruth Norman.

Norman Hallo.

Ruth I'm ready.

Norman Right. Want a spoonful of jam? That's all there is. 'Till Reg arrives with a blazing sliced loaf.

Ruth I can wait.

Norman Okay.

Ruth Good morning, Sarah. (*No reply*) Guess who isn't speaking to me this morning. I'll be in the sitting-room, Norman, when you can tear yourself away from Mother Doom here.

Norman Coming.

Ruth goes out to the house

Sarah Reg gets home about half past six in the evening on weekdays.

Norman Busy man.

Sarah If you feel like giving me a ring any time. I'm usually tied to the house. I don't get out much.

Norman I'd make you happy, Sarah.

Sarah Yes.

Norman 'Bye-bye.

Norman goes out to the house, eating the last of his toast

Sarah looks thoughtful. She gives a pleased grunt

Reg enters with the empty toast-rack

Reg Dear oh dear. (*He sits at the table*)

Sarah Have you got it?

Reg What?

Sarah I thought you were going to make yourself some toast.

Reg Oh, I don't know. I looked at the grill and I looked at the loaf and I thought—that's a lot of effort for a piece of toast. I'll make do with this piece.

Sarah Well, I've finished.

Reg Tea's cold as well now. Not my day, is it?

Sarah No, I don't think it is.

Annie and Tom enter from the house

Annie Look who's here.
Reg I told you he was here.
Tom 'Morning. 'Morning, Sarah.
Sarah Hallo, Tom. Bright and early.
Tom Yes. I didn't sleep very well, I'm afraid.
Annie Just tea, Tom?
Tom Just a cup, thank you.
Reg It's stone cold.
Annie Well, I'll hot it up. That's easy enough.

Annie goes out with the teapot

Tom I wanted to apologize for last night.
Sarah What?
Tom Well—lashing out—Norman. Totally lost control. Feel very embarrassed about it.
Sarah Nobody hurt fortunately.
Tom No, I didn't get a very good swing. Bit rusty.
Sarah Just as well.
Tom Yes. Rather.
Sarah I'm glad you've come back, anyway.
Tom I'm afraid I don't seem to be able to keep away.
Sarah It'll be nice for Annie with us all going.
Tom I'm only here for a second. I'm actually on my way to a call. Horse. Fetlock.
Sarah Oh.
Tom Not too serious. She can wait.
Reg Let her stand on three legs for a bit. (*He laughs*)
Tom No, she can stand all right.
Sarah Well, I hope you'll look after Annie for us.
Tom Oh, yes, I'll do my best. I think she really looks after me. (*He laughs*).
Sarah Yes, well, you mustn't let it get too one-sided, must you?
Tom What? Oh. No. I do help . . .
Sarah Yes. It depends what you do though, doesn't it?
Tom I did the ceiling in the kitchen. And . . .
Sarah No, I meant a little more than that.
Reg I thought we were in a hurry.
Sarah Oh. Yes.
Reg Will we see you at Christmas, Tom? Or are you going to Scotland again?
Tom Probably.
Reg Oh, well. Sometime. All the best.

Annie enters with the teapot

Annie Are you off?
Sarah Yes, we must. (*She rises*)
Annie Okay. I'll come and see you've got everything. Here you are, Tom I topped it up. (*She puts the pot on the table*)

Tom Thanks.
Annie Be back in a sec.
Reg 'Bye.
Sarah Good-bye, Tom.
Tom 'Bye.

Sarah, Annie and Reg go out

Tom sits alone. He puts a plate in front of himself, then sees the empty toast-rack. He pours the tea. It is practically white

Tom Oh. Oh well . . . (*He sits and sings to himself. Tom, on his own, is amazingly cheerful. He amuses himself by arranging the things on the table in a strange secret pattern of his own*)

At length, Annie returns

Annie All right? (*She sits at the table*)
Tom Fine. All gone have they?
Annie Just about. Norman and Ruth seem to be having trouble starting their car.
Tom Oh, should I . . . (*He half rises*)
Annie No. Enjoy your tea.
Tom Oh, yes.
Annie Have you got any tea in there or is it just milk?
Tom No, it is tea. Bit anaemic.
Annie I'll make some more in a minute. Quite a week-end.
Tom Yes.
Annie I've behaved very badly. I'm sorry.
Tom No. It's me . . .
Annie No. (*Pause*) Tom . . .
Tom Um?
Annie Has your—opinion of me gone down as a result of this week-end? I mean, do you think less of me?
Tom Good Lord, no.
Annie You still—like me?
Tom Oh, yes. Of course I do.
Annie You'll still come round?
Tom You bet. (*He laughs*) Once you've improved the tea, anyway.
Annie The only reason I said I would go with Norman, you see, was—I suddenly felt very lonely.
Tom Yes, I understand. It's all right. We all get lonely. If you're lonely again and I'm not here, why don't you give me a ring?
Annie (*picking up a dessert-spoon and twiddling it in her fingers*) This is a very big house, you see. Most of the time it's just Mother and me here. We'll have to sell it eventually, it's ridiculous.
Tom I wouldn't do that.
Annie We'll have to. We'll have to move somewhere smaller. Perhaps in Essex. Or Norfolk. Or Northumberland.

Tom Bit off the beaten track.
Annie Yes.
Tom Wouldn't see much of me.
Annie No.
Tom Well, if you do sell it, make sure you give me first refusal, won't you?
(*He gets up*) Well, I'd better go and see to my horse.
Annie Yes. Go and see to your horse.

Annie turns the side plate in front of her upside down on the table. She bangs on it deliberately with a spoon. A regular sort of rhythm which, although not fast, grows in intensity until the plate breaks

Tom (*watching her curiously*) What on earth are you doing?
Annie Breaking things. Breaking things for breakfast.
Tom (*laughs awkwardly*) Careful of splinters.

Norman rushes in, in his coat and hat

Norman Disaster! We cannot start it.
Tom Oh goodness. Want a hand?
Norman Need one of these ex-boxers to give it a shove.
Tom Right. My pleasure. Probably see you later, Annie.
Annie Yes.

Tom goes to the garden

Norman is about to follow when he notices Annie and the plate

Norman What are you doing? Don't tell me, you've finally run out of food. I told you you'd get round to eating the plates eventually. Now the nicest way to eat a plate—is spread it with a thin layer of jam and then pour custard all over the . . .

Annie flies at Norman and clings on to him

Annie Oh, Norman . . .
Norman Only you want to make sure it's thick custard.
Annie (*muffled*) I want . . .
Norman Eh?
Annie I want . . .
Norman I can't hear you. What?
Annie (*in a wail*) I want to go to East Grinstead.
Norman (*soothing her*) All right. Fine. I'll take you. I'll take you.
Annie (*tearfully*) Will you?
Norman Just say the word. Come on now, don't cry. I'll make you happy. Don't worry. I'll make you happy.

Norman hugs her to him. Annie clings on. Norman looks towards the window, then out front, smiling happily

CURTAIN

FURNITURE AND PROPERTY LIST

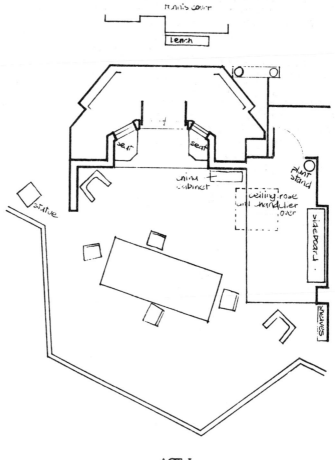

ACT I

SCENE 1

On stage: Large dining table. *On it:* 6 roses
4 matching dining chairs
2 easy chairs with antimacassars and cushions
China cabinet. *On it:* table lamp

Standard lamp
Plant stand and plant
Sideboard. *On top:* round tray with 6 glasses, cruet set, biscuit tin
    containing water biscuits. *In cupboard:* 4 side plates in a pile
    (Act I), 6 side plates in a pile (Act II), 6 wine glasses, 4 rush mats.
    In top drawer: 3 tray cloths, duster, 8 starched damask table napkins.
    In cutlery drawer: 6 knives, 6 forks, 6 dessert spoons. *In bottom
    drawer:* 6 place mats
Garden bench in garden
Shelves with china
Carpet

Off stage: Vase with water (**Annie**)
       Waste-paper basket (**Reg**)
       Wine glass half-full of parsnip wine (**Tom**)
       Dustpan and brush (**Annie**)
       Jar of salad cream (**Sarah**)

       Bottle of home-made carrot wine (**Tom**)
       Tray with 4 plates of salad (**Annie**)

Personal: **Annie:** handkerchief
       Sarah: handbag with handkerchief and compact
       Annie, Sarah, Reg, Tom: wrist watches

SCENE 2

Strike: Everything from table

Off stage: Tray with 4 side plates, 4 knives, toast-rack, jam, marmalade, napkin,
       butter dish, 2 jam spoons (**Sarah**)
       Tray with 4 cups, saucers and teaspoons, sugar bowl and spoon,
       large jug of milk, hot-water jug, teapot, rush mat (**Annie**)
       Packet of Puffa Puffa Rice (**Sarah**)
       Packet of cornflakes (**Sarah**)
       3 cereal bowls and spoons (**Sarah**)

Personal: **Ruth:** handbag with compact, handkerchief, car keys
       Ruth: wrist watch

ACT II

SCENE 1

Strike: Everything from table

Set: Cruet and biscuit tin on sideboard
       6 glasses on tray on sideboard

Off stage: 4 knives, 4 forks, 4 spoons (**Annie**)
       Duster (**Sarah**)

Apron (**Sarah**)
Odd dining chair (**Reg**)
Low chair (**Reg**)
Bottle of home-made parsnip wine and corkscrew (**Sarah**)
Tray with 4 plates of sparse salad (**Sarah**)
Saucepan with stew, ladle, with 2 tea towels round handles (**Annie**)
6 soup plates (**Reg**)

SCENE 2

Strike: Everything from table

Off stage: Tray with 6 side plates, 6 cups, 6 saucers and teaspoons, milk. jug,
              hot-water jug, jar of jam, jar of marmalade, rush mat, butter
              dish, napkin, 6 knives, 1 dessert spoon, toast-rack, with 3 pieces
              of toast, sugar bowl and spoon, teapot (**Annie**)
              Hot water to refill teapot

LIGHTING PLOT

Property fittings required: standard lamp, table lamp, pendant (dressing only)
Interior. A dining-room. The same scene throughout

ACT I, SCENE 1. Evening
To open: Effect of early evening sunshine
No cues

ACT I, SCENE 2. Morning
To open: Effect of bright summer morning
No cues

ACT II, SCENE 1. Evening
To open: Effect of late evening light, summer
No cues

ACT II, SCENE 2. Morning
To open: As Act I, Scene 2
No cues

EFFECTS PLOT

ACT I

Scene 1

Cue 1   **Reg:** "Hardly at all."   (Page 17)
         Record off stage of Richard Tauber singing "Girls were made to
         Love and Kiss", continue for a few moments, then fade

Cue 2   **Sarah:** ". . . a civilized meal."   (Page 19)
         Bring up record as above until Curtain falls

Scene 2

No cues

ACT II

Scene 1

No cues

Scene 2

No cues